SPECTRUM®
LANGUAGE ARTS

Grade 7

CREDITS
Editor: Catherine Malaski
Cover Design: J.J. Giddings, Nick Pearson, Lynne Schwaner
Interior Design: Lynne Schwaner
Illustrations: Nick Pearson, Robin Krantz, J.J. Giddings, Morgan Burnside, Lynne Schwaner

Spectrum®
An imprint of Carson Dellosa Education
PO Box 35665
Greensboro, NC 27425 USA

ISBN 978-1-4838-7141-7
02-295241151

Table of Contents Grade 7

Table of Contents Grade 7

Spectrum Introduction

For more than 20 years, Spectrum® workbooks have been the solution for helping students meet and exceed learning goals. Each title in the Spectrum workbook series offers grade-appropriate instruction and reinforcement in an effective sequence for learning success.

Spectrum partners with you in supporting your student's educational journey every step of the way! This book will help them navigate seventh grade language arts and will give you the support you need to make sure your student learns everything they need to know. Inside you will find:

Chapter Introductions

These introductions provide useful information about the chapter. Including:

Background Information

This introductory text provides you with background information about specific skills taught in the chapter.

Helpful Definitions

These terms either appear in the chapter or are important for the skills being taught.

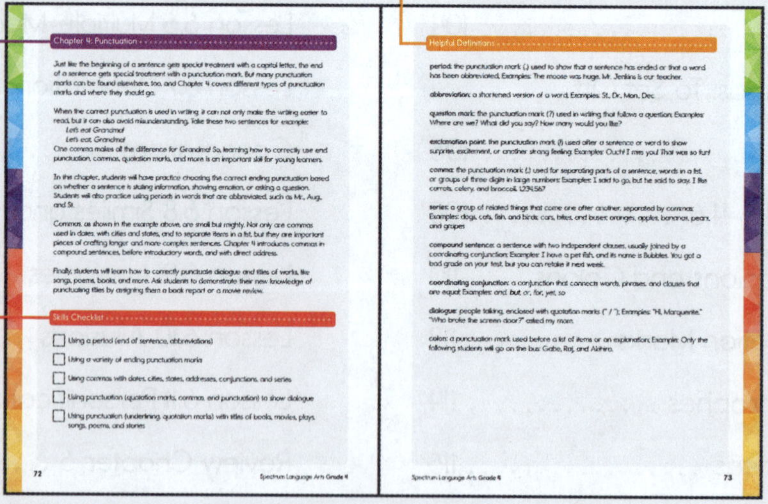

Chapter 4: Punctuation

Just like the beginning of a sentence gets special treatment with a capital letter, the end of a sentence gets special treatment with a punctuation mark. But many punctuation marks can be found elsewhere, too, and Chapter 4 covers different types of punctuation marks and where they should go.

When the correct punctuation is used in writing, it can not only make the writing easier to read, but it can also avoid misunderstanding. Take these two sentences for example:

Let's eat Grandma!
Let's eat, Grandma!

One comma makes all the difference for Grandma! So, learning how to correctly use end punctuation, commas, quotation marks, and more is an important skill for young learners.

In this chapter, students will have practice choosing the correct ending punctuation based on whether a sentence is stating information, showing emotion, or asking a question. Students will also practice using periods in words that are abbreviated, such as Mr., Aug., and St.

Commas, as shown in the example above, are small but mighty. Not only are commas used in dates, with cities and states, and to separate items in a list, but they are important pieces of crafting longer and more complex sentences. Chapter 4 introduces commas in compound sentences, before introductory words, and with direct address.

Finally, students will learn how to correctly punctuate dialogue and titles of works, like songs, poems, books, and more. Ask students to demonstrate their new knowledge of punctuating titles by assigning them a book report or a movie review.

Skills Checklist

- ☐ Using a period (end of sentence, abbreviations)
- ☐ Using a variety of ending punctuation marks
- ☐ Using commas with dates, cities, states, addresses, conjunctions, and series
- ☐ Using punctuation (quotation marks, commas, and punctuation) to show dialogue
- ☐ Using punctuation (underlining, quotation marks) with titles of books, movies, plays, songs, poems, and stories

72 Spectrum Language Arts Grade 4

Helpful Definitions

period: the punctuation mark (.) used to show that a sentence has ended or that a word has been abbreviated. Examples: The moose was huge. Mr. Jenkins is our teacher.

abbreviation: a shortened version of a word. Examples: St., Dr., Mon., Dec.

question mark: the punctuation mark (?) used in writing that follows a question. Examples: Where are we? What did you say? How many would you like?

exclamation point: the punctuation mark (!) used after a sentence or word to show surprise, excitement, or another strong feeling. Examples: Ouch! I miss you! That was so fun!

comma: the punctuation mark (,) used for separating parts of a sentence, words in a list, or groups of three digits in large numbers. Examples: I said to go, but he said to stay. I like carrots, celery, and broccoli. 1,234,567

series: a group of related things that come one after another, separated by commas. Examples: dogs, cats, fish, and birds; cars, bikes, and buses; oranges, apples, bananas, pears, and grapes

compound sentence: a sentence with two independent clauses, usually joined by a coordinating conjunction. Examples: I have a pet fish, and its name is Bubbles. You got a bad grade on your test, but you can retake it next week.

coordinating conjunction: a conjunction that connects words, phrases, and clauses that are equal. Examples: and, **but**, or, for, yet, so

dialogue: people talking, enclosed with quotation marks (" / "). Examples: "Hi, Marguerite." "Who broke the screen door?" asked my mom.

colon: a punctuation mark used before a list of items or an explanation. Example: Only the following students will go on the bus: Gabe, Raj, and Akhira.

Spectrum Language Arts Grade 4 73

Skills Checklist

This checklist helps ensure your student is practicing grade-level skills.

Lessons

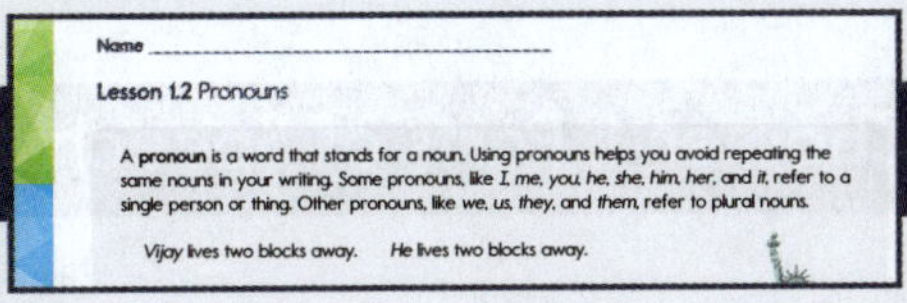
Name ____________________

Lesson 1.2 Pronouns

A **pronoun** is a word that stands for a noun. Using pronouns helps you avoid repeating the same nouns in your writing. Some pronouns, like *I, me, you, he, she, him, her,* and *it,* refer to a single person or thing. Other pronouns, like *we, us, they,* and *them,* refer to plural nouns.

Vijay lives two blocks away. He lives two blocks away.

These pages begin with a definition, step-by-step instructions where needed, and examples, followed by independent practice.

Enrichment

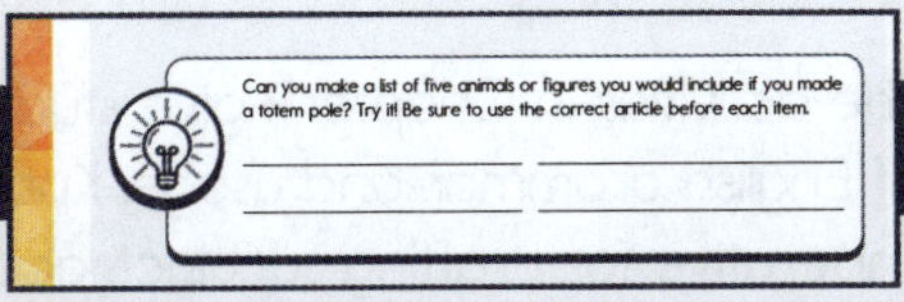
Can you make a list of five animals or figures you would include if you made a totem pole? Try it! Be sure to use the correct article before each item.

These problems appear throughout the book. They allow your student to dig deeper and apply the skill they learned in a different way than it is practiced on the page. The two types of problems will ask your student to think critically and explain reasoning.

Chapter Reviews

Name ____________________

Chapter 1 Review

Answer the following questions.

These end-of-chapter reviews go over the skills learned within each chapter and can be used to gauge your student's progress.

Learning Checkpoints

Name ____________________

Learning Checkpoint Chapters 1–3

Circle the letter of the sentence that is capitalized correctly.

These reviews break up the book into halfway points to prepare your student for the final test.

Final Test

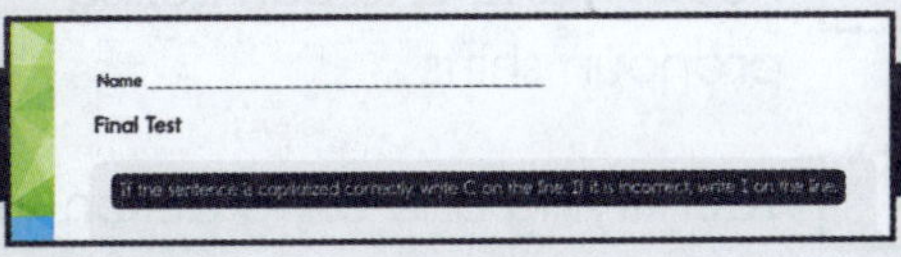
Name ____________________

Final Test

If the sentence is capitalized correctly, write C on the line. If it is incorrect, write I on the line.

This test covers the skills learned in the book. Use this comprehensive test to assess what your student has learned and to identify what they still need to work on.

Answer Key

The answers to the lessons, reviews, and tests are provided in an answer key.

Chapter 1: Parts of Speech

We begin this *Spectrum Language Arts* book for Grade 7 with a focus on the parts of speech. Chapter 1 builds on students' already established knowledge of nouns, pronouns, verbs, adjectives, conjunctions, interjections, and prepositions.

The activities in Chapter 1 give students valuable practice in demonstrating their command of English grammar and usage. Knowing how to correctly use the parts of speech is imperative for crafting succinct, accurate writing that is also interesting to read. This chapter will show students that using variety in their writing is not only fun and easy, but it also adds interest to sentences, paragraphs, and stories.

Skills Checklist

- [ ] Identifying and using common, proper, collective, and abstract nouns
- [ ] Identifying and using singular and plural possessives
- [ ] Identifying and using appositives
- [ ] Identifying and using subject, object, relative, intensive, reflexive, and indefinite pronouns
- [ ] Recognizing and correcting pronoun shifts
- [ ] Identifying and using action verbs
- [ ] Recognizing and using correct subject-verb agreement
- [ ] Recognizing and using transitive, intransitive, helping, and linking verbs
- [ ] Identifying and using gerunds, participles, and infinitives
- [ ] Recognizing and using past, present, future, progressive, and perfect verb tenses
- [ ] Recognizing and using different types of adjectives
- [ ] Identifying and using prepositions and prepositional phrases
- [ ] Recognizing and using conjunctions and interjections

Helpful Definitions

collective noun: a singular word that represents a group; Examples: *herd, family*

abstract noun: a noun that names an idea, quality, or state of being; Example: *honesty*

possessive: a noun or pronoun that shows possession; Examples: *Jim's car, his car*

appositive: a noun or pronoun set next to another noun or pronoun to identify it; Example: *My teacher, Ms. Pho, is nice.*

subject pronoun: a pronoun that replaces the subject of a sentence; Example: *She left today.*

object pronoun: a pronoun that replaces the noun that is the receiver of the action in a sentence; Example: *Neil gave a gift to her.*

relative pronoun: a pronoun used to introduce a relative clause; Examples: *who, which, that*

intensive pronoun: a word ending in -self or -selves, typically used with a noun or pronoun; Examples: *herself, themselves*

reflexive pronoun: a pronoun that refers back to a noun or pronoun in the same sentence; Examples: *myself, himself*

indefinite pronoun: a pronoun that does not refer to a specific person, place, or thing; Examples: *anyone, everything*

pronoun shift: when a writer begins with one type of pronoun and suddenly shifts to another; Example: *If someone calls, tell them I am not home.*

subject-verb agreement: when a singular subject is paired with a singular verb and a plural subject is paired with a plural verb; Examples: *dog chases, dogs chase*

transitive verb: an action verb that requires an object to show who or what was acted on; Example: *I play the piano.*

intransitive verb: an action verb that does not need a direct object; Example: *How fast can you play?*

helping verb: a verb that helps to form tenses of main verbs; Examples: *am, are, was, were*

linking verb: a verb that does not show action; it links the subject of the sentence to what is said about the subject; Examples: *is, was, sounds, looks*

gerund: the noun form of a verb that ends in -ing; Example: *Swimming is fun!*

participle: the adjective form of a verb; Example: *running water*

infinitive: a form of verb that can be used as a noun, adjective, or adverb usually preceded by the word *to*; Examples: *to sleep, to write*

proper adjective: an adjective formed from a proper noun; always capitalized; Example: *French fries*

preposition: a word or group of words that show the relationship between a noun or pronoun and another word in the sentence; Examples: *between, on, under*

coordinate conjunction: connects words, phrases, or clauses; Examples: *and, but, or*

correlative conjunctions: pairs of conjunctions; Examples: *both/and, either/or*

interjection: a one- or two-word phrase used to express surprise or strong emotion; Examples: *Hey! Ouch!*

Name ______________________________

Lesson 1.1 Common and Proper Nouns

Common nouns name people, places, things, and ideas.

People	Places	Things	Ideas
author, neighbor, doctor, parent, friend, hostess	city, bus stop, apartment, classroom, marina	government, flood, tornado, test, violin, picture	joy, freedom, fear, excitement, honesty

Proper nouns name specific people, places, and things. Proper nouns are capitalized.

People	Places	Things
Gabriella, Mr. Martinez, Dr. Cottrell	Tucson, Acadia National Park, Rome	Peppy's Pizza, the Gilded Age

Underline the common noun(s) and circle the proper noun(s) in each sentence.

1. The United States is the third largest country in the world.
2. It is bordered by the Atlantic Ocean on the east and the Pacific Ocean on the west.
3. Canada and Mexico are countries that border the United States.
4. The bald eagle is the national bird of the United States.
5. Two major mountain ranges in the United States are the Rocky Mountains and the Appalachian Mountains.
6. The hottest place in the country, and on Earth, is Death Valley.

Can you think of a favorite place you've visited in the United States? Write it down.

The Poconos

Name ______________________________

Lesson 1.1 Common and Proper Nouns

Correct the mistakes in the use of common and proper nouns using proofreading marks.

m (triple underline) capitalize a letter	M (slash) lowercase a letter

1. Every Winter we visit my Grandpa in Sarasota, florida.
2. We leave around christmas and stay until new Year's Day.
3. Our favorite Thing to do with Him is swim in the gulf of Mexico.
4. We take our Fishing poles to siesta key to try to catch Striped fish.
5. We always have to eat Shrimp at suzi's Shrimp Shack before we come home.

For each common noun, write a proper noun.

	Common Noun	Proper Noun
6.	city	NYC
7.	neighbor	Henry
8.	teacher	Mrs. Stone
9.	pet	Marvel
10.	car	Subaru

Name ______________________________

Lesson 1.2 Collective and Abstract Nouns

Collective nouns are used to describe groups of specific animals, people, or things.
A group of sheep is a **flock**.
A group of musicians is a **band**.
A group of soldiers is an **army**.

A collective noun refers to more than one thing, but it acts as a singular noun when used in a sentence. So a singular verb must be used.
Incorrect: The **flock are** grazing in the pasture.
Correct: The **flock is** grazing in the pasture.

Abstract nouns describe ideas that can be perceived with the five senses rather than people, places, or things.

joy **despair** **brilliance** **bravery** **pride**

Match each plural noun in the left column with its singular collective noun in the right column.

1. grapes	team
2. flowers	swarm
3. singers	galaxy
4. stars	pair
5. cards	choir
6. bees	range
7. athletes	fleet
8. people	deck
9. shoes	crowd
10. ships	bunch
11. mountains	bouquet

Name ______________________________

Lesson 1.2 Collective and Abstract Nouns

Circle the verb in each sentence that correctly completes the sentence. On the line, write **C** if the underlined noun is a collective noun. Write **A** if it is an abstract noun.

1. __C__ The team (is, are) practicing every day before the playoff game.
2. __C__ The crowd (cheer, cheers) as the singer takes the stage.
3. __A__ As Marissa received her diploma, the feeling that her mom felt (was, were) sheer pride.
4. __A__ The scientist's brilliance (was, were) obvious to everyone.
5. __C__ My grandma's neighborhood (has, have) a pool to swim in.
6. __C__ The crew (prepare, prepares) the ship for its year-long journey to the Baltic Sea.

Can you use a collective and an abstract noun in one sentence? Try it!

____

____

Name ______________________________

Lesson 1.3 Singular and Plural Possessives

A **possessive noun** shows ownership.

To make a **singular noun** possessive, add an apostrophe and an **s** (**'s**).
the **boy's** coat

To make a **plural noun** possessive, add an apostrophe after the **s** (**'**).
the **boys'** coats

To make an **irregular plural noun** possessive, add an apostrophe and an **s** (**'s**).
the **children's** coats

Rewrite each sentence with the correct possessive form of the bold word.

1. The **womans** baby was crying.
   The women's baby was crying.
2. Five **horses** manes were braided.
   Five horses' manes were braided
3. The **cherries** stems were hard to pull off.
   The cherry's stems were hard to pull of
4. My **neighbors** garage door was open all night.
   My neighbor's garage door was open all night
5. The baseball and softball **teams** uniforms were freshly laundered.
   ____
6. A **dragonflys** wings are transparent.
   ____

Name ______________________________

Lesson 1.3 Singular and Plural Possessives

Look at the bold word in each sentence. On the line, write **PL** if the word is a plural noun, **SP** if the word is a singular possessive, or **PP** if the word is a plural possessive.

1. PL Marine **biologists** travel to Belize to scuba dive down to reefs.
2. PP Marine **biologists'** equipment can include microscopes, test tubes, cameras, and tracking devices.
3. PL Coral **reefs** are home to starfish, clownfish, sea anemone, and so much more.
4. PP Endangered **species'** lives depend on reefs for survival.
5. PL **Reefs** give animals protection against flooding and storm surge.
6. PP Marine biologists also study **turtles'** habitats.
7. PL Many **turtles** live in shallow water in bays, lagoons, and estuaries.
8. PP **Turtles'** nests can be found in warm sand.
9. SP In a **turtle's** nest you might find up to 100 eggs!
10. SP A marine **biologist's** job is exciting and fascinating.

Write three sentences using the words below. Use each word in a different sentence.

seahorse	seahorse's	seahorses'

11. The Seahorse was swimming in its tank.
12. The seahorse's scales looked pretty as people watched it.
13. The Aquarium alltogether had 23 Seahorses' in it.

Name ______________________________

Lesson 1.4 Appositives

An **appositive** is a noun or phrase that renames another noun in a sentence. The appositive offers more information about the noun.

Goldie, **our goldfish,** has lived in my aquarium for over two years.

The phrase **our goldfish** is an appositive that renames **Goldie.**

When the appositive is non-essential, or not necessary to the sentence, it should have a comma before and after it. In the example above, you can remove the appositive and the sentence still makes sense.

Read each sentence below. Underline the appositives. Circle the nouns they rename.

1. SailGP, an extreme sailboat race, is thrilling to watch.
2. The FIFA World Cup, which started in 1930, is watched by millions every year.
3. The Cricket World Cup, played once every four years, started in England.
4. Wimbledon, the most prestigious tennis tournament in the world, is played on grass courts.
5. The Tour de France, held in France and neighboring countries, is 23 days of cycling.
6. The Summer Olympics, held every four years, has over 300 sporting events.
7. It is believed that rugby, a game that combines football and soccer, originated in England.
8. The Daytona 500, which is 500 miles long, is 200 laps around the track.

Explain why appositives can be good to include when writing sentences.

____

____

Name ______________________________

Lesson 1.4 Appositives

Rewrite each sentence by adding an appositive that gives more information about the noun or pronoun it renames. Underline the appositive.

1. Maria is teaching Ellie how to play the piano.

____

2. My favorite side dish was a choice on the menu.

____

3. Mr. Baumgarten handed me my test.

____

4. Chloe chased me until her owner called her name.

____

5. Ronald Reagan was governor of California from 1967 to 1975.

____

6. My aunt and I saw Wicked at the theater.

____

These sentences contain appositives, but they are not punctuated correctly. Add the commas where needed.

7. Burlington the largest city in Vermont is on Lake Champlain.

8. Mrs. Smithe a loving teacher is retiring at the end of the year.

Name ______________________________

Lesson 1.5 Pronouns

A **pronoun** is a word used in place of a noun. A **subject pronoun** can be used as the subject of a sentence. It can be singular (**I, you, he, she, it**) or plural (**we, you, they**).

She rode her new bike to school.

An **object pronoun** is the object of a verb or preposition. It can also be singular (**me, you, him, her, it**) or plural (**us, you, them**).

Mr. Robson asked **us** to collect the papers.

A **possessive pronoun** shows possession. Singular possessive pronouns are **my, mine, your, yours, his, her, hers,** and **its**, and plural possessive pronouns are **our, ours, your, yours, their,** and **theirs**.

Their street was being repaved.

Read each sentence below and decide how the bold pronoun is used. On the line, write **SP** for subject pronoun, **OP** for object pronoun, or **PP** for possessive pronoun.

1. PP Amanda and **her** dad like to explore caves together.

2. SP **They** first started spelunking, or caving, when Amanda was thirteen.

3. OP Amanda's grandparents bought **her** some gear for Christmas.

4. SP "**We** hope you love caving," said Amanda's grandparents.

5. Op Amanda's dad said, "Spelunking has introduced **me** to the beauty of the natural world."

6. PP Amanda and her dad have traveled to four different states to pursue **their** hobby.

Name ______________________________

Lesson 1.5 Pronouns

Choose the correct pronoun that completes each sentence.

1. ____________ opened the door and the passengers exited the plane.

   a. Them

   b. He

   c. Us

2. Cherie made a birdhouse and painted ____________ yellow.

   a. it

   b. we

   c. him

3. Adam met ____________ at the movie at 7:30pm.

   a. we

   b. me

   c. I

4. Ginny promised to take ____________ for ice cream.

   a. them

   b. we

   c. their

5. ____________ and I have had many sleepovers.

   a. Her

   b. We

   c. She

6. We ordered burgers and ____________ were cold.

   a. it

   b. them

   c. they

Name ______________________________

Lesson 1.6 Relative Pronouns

Relative pronouns introduce relative clauses. These dependent clauses give more information about the subject of the sentence. **Who, whom, whose, that**, and **which** are all relative pronouns.

The lasagna **that** Grey's mom made was good!
That's the lady **whose** daughter is in my class.

Underline the relative pronoun in each sentence. Circle the relative clause.

1. The ball that I threw was heavy.

2. My teacher, whom I like, is retiring next month.

3. The woman whose car was hit was crying.

4. The restaurant that was going to close is now staying open.

5. We are taking a trip to Norfolk, which is in Virginia.

6. The little redheaded boy, who was wearing a baseball hat, looked sad.

7. Anacondas, which live in the rainforest, are the largest snake.

8. The black dog, whose ball went into the water, stood on the river's edge.

Explain how a relative pronoun clause adds to a sentence's meaning.

____

____

Name ____________________

Lesson 1.6 Relative Pronouns

The relative pronouns **that** and **which** have different uses. **That** is followed by necessary information. **Which** is followed by additional information.

I saw a dog **that** looked just like my dog! The party, **which** was a surprise, was fun.

Complete each sentence with either that or which.

1. The sink that is plugged needs to be fixed.
2. I put my laptop in my backpack, which is waterproof.
3. The truck that had a flat tire had pulled over.
4. The last book that I read was The Secret Garden.

The relative pronouns **who** and **whom** have different uses too. **Who** is used as the subject of a sentence. **Whom** is used as the object of the sentence.

Complete each sentence with either who or whom.

5. Who bought the bike you were selling?
6. My neighbor whom I talk to is so nice.
7. Pho is the boy who has a broken leg.
8. Do you know whom she looks like?

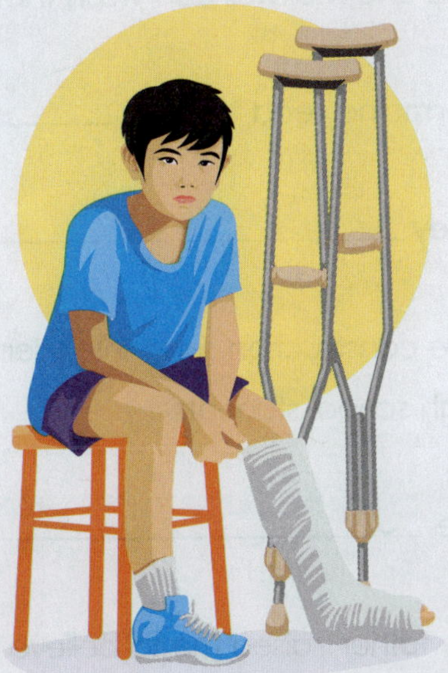

Name ________________________________

Lesson 1.7 Intensive and Reflexive Pronouns

Intensive and **reflexive pronouns** are pronouns that end in **-self** or **-selves.** The way the pronoun is used determines whether it is intensive or reflexive.

Intensive pronouns usually appear right after the subject of a sentence. They emphasize the subject.

I myself have seen the Northern Lights.

He himself went back to the store to look for his keys.

Reflexive pronouns appear elsewhere in the sentence and refer back to the subject.

The bird bathed **itself** in the new bird bath.

We fed **ourselves** with the fresh fish we caught.

Intensive and Reflexive Pronouns:

myself, yourself, himself/herself, ourselves, themselves

Complete each sentence below with an intensive or reflexive pronoun.

1. I Myself like to take bike rides around the lake.

2. Kyrie himself planned a great surprise party.

3. You and Maxwell can wash the car yourself if it's not raining.

4. Jermaine read to himself before turning his light off.

5. They themselves were stuck in traffic on the way to the theater.

6. The construction superintendent himself gave advice to the high school students.

7. We ourselves all cleaned our grandparents' house.

8. My father raised me to believe in Myself.

Name ______________________________

Lesson 1.7 Intensive and Reflexive Pronouns

The intensive and reflexive pronouns are in bold. Underline the subject the pronoun refers to.

1. Two days before the garage sale, Keisha **herself** carried ten boxes up from the basement.

2. Her brother and sister helped **themselves** to the things they wanted to keep.

3. Lamonte **himself** found a wagon he used to ride in when he was little.

4. Myla set aside some favorite books **herself**.

5. On the day of the sale, the garage **itself** was packed with customers.

6. The Murio family bought **themselves** some family board games.

7. "Did you **yourself** collect all these baseball cards?" Mr. Patel asked Lamonte.

8. "Those were my grandpa's cards. I'm not into baseball **myself**," he said.

Can you write two sentences using intensive and reflexive pronouns? Try it.

1. ______________________________

____

2. ______________________________

____

Name ______________________________

Lesson 1.8 Indefinite Pronouns

Indefinite pronouns are pronouns that do not specifically name the noun that comes before it.

another	anybody	anyone	anything	each
everybody	everyone	everything	nobody	none
no one	nothing	one	somebody	someone

I was talking to **anyone** who would listen.
Each of my friends lives in an apartment.
No one understood what happened to make her mad.

Most indefinite pronouns are singular, but the following are plural:
both **few** **many** **others** **several**

Many otters at the zoo were playing in the water.
Few people like anchovies on their pizza.

Some indefinite pronouns, such as **all, any, more, most,** and **some**, are either singular or plural, depending on their meaning in the sentence.

All will become clear in the final act of the play.
All of the bison in the area were standing in the road.

Underline the indefinite pronoun in each sentence.

1. Not everyone likes the hustle and bustle of a big city.
2. If there is anything I know for sure, it's that my dog is the greatest.
3. Quinn shovels the Chan's driveway when no one is home in the winter.
4. Somebody spilled ice cream all over the park bench.
5. The two beds had been taken by others, so I slept on the couch.
6. None of the mice were tempted by the cheese in the trap.

Name ______________________________

Lesson 1.8 Indefinite Pronouns

Circle the correct form of the verb shown in parentheses. Then underline the indefinite pronoun.

1. If everyone (clean, cleans) up, it'll go faster.
2. All (was, were) lost as the drone fell from the sky into the water.
3. Nothing (is, are) impossible if you believe in yourself.
4. Both Seth and Carmine (is, are) spelling bee champions.
5. Somebody (like, likes) to leave anonymous notes in my locker.
6. Everyone (has, have) a responsibility to take care of our planet.
7. If anybody (disagree, disagrees) with my opinion, I'd love to talk about it.
8. Either option (give, gives) us a quick way around the traffic jam.

Can you choose two indefinite pronouns and write a sentence for each one? Try it. At the end of each sentence, write **S** if the pronoun is singular or **P** if it is plural.

1. ______________________________

____

2. ______________________________

____

Name ______________________________

Lesson 1.9 Pronoun Shifts

A **pronoun shift** happens when a writer changes pronouns in the middle of a sentence or paragraph. This can confuse the reader.

In this example, the writer changes from **they** (third-person plural) to **you** (second-person singular):

Incorrect: Our neighbors thought **they** could put up a fence, but **you** can't do that in our neighborhood.

Correct: Our neighbors thought **they** could put up a fence, but **they** can't do that in our neighborhood.

In this example, **trees** (a plural noun) and **it** (third-person singular pronoun) do not agree.

Incorrect: Large **trees** were cut down because **it** cast too much shade over our yard.

Correct: Large **trees** were cut down because **they** cast too much shade over our yard.

Rewrite each sentence to correct the pronoun shift.

1. A cartoonist must practice every day if they want to get better.

____

2. Our black and white poodle was the spitting image of their parents.

____

3. Steven and Linh asked us if we wanted to go swimming with him.

____

4. A police officer helped me with my flat tire, and they showed me how to do it myself if it happens again.

____

5. A good fisherman will wait quietly until they feel a tug on the line.

____

6. Most kids understand that eating healthy is good for you.

____

Name ____

Lesson 1.9 Pronoun Shifts

Circle the pronoun that correctly completes the sentence.

1. The teachers met after school and (it, they) voted to give students an extra recess on Fridays.
2. When my brother and I go camping, (he, we) fish every day.
3. The twins were scared because (we, they) saw the big storm coming on the radar.
4. The bald eagles at the zoo are a fan favorite even though (it, they) just sit in their nest.
5. For walks to school on snowy days, make sure Chloe has a hat and gloves with (her, them).
6. A baby giraffe faces challenges in the wild, but (it, you) learns quickly how to stay safe.
7. The painters forgot their brushes, so (we, they) quickly drove home to get them.
8. After much anticipation, the new splash pad is finally done and (it, they) will open on Monday.

9. The directions for the furniture were printed so small I could hardly read (it, them).
10. The girls chose to wear the same outfit to school, and (you, they) took pictures for fun.

Why do you think it is important to have agreement between pronouns in a sentence? Explain.

____

____

Name ________________________________

Review Lessons 1.1–1.9

Identify the type of each underlined noun using the key in the box. Write the letter of your answer on the line following each underlined noun.

a. common noun **b. proper noun** **c. collective noun** **d. abstract noun**

1. My family ________ is moving to Beaverton ________, Oregon, so my mom can work for Nike ________.
2. One of Andre's ________ favorite memories of his childhood ________ is visiting relatives ________ in Italy ________ and being part of a cooking class ________ where he learned to make lasagna ________.
3. When we went to the Screamin' Coasters Amusement Park ________ last August ________, my mom could see the excitement ________ and fear ________ on our faces when we walked into the park.
4. For our camping trip ________, we packed a tent, a deck ________ of cards, fishing poles, raincoats, and a pair ________ of pie irons.

In the sentences below, circle singular possessives, underline plurals, and underline plural possessives twice.

5. Mr. Meyer's students are entering their art pieces in a citywide art contest.
6. The students' parents will drive them to the park in the city.
7. RayAnne's piece, a rendering of the city skyline, took her two weeks to draw.
8. The Lehman twins' portrait of a stray dog won first place.

One sentence above contains an appositive. Can you find it? Put a star next to the sentence.

Name ______________________________

Review Lessons 1.1–1.9

Underline the word that best completes each sentence below.

9. Even though Rusty and Rex are both redheads, (them, they) do not look alike.

10. I (myself, yourself) have given up eating meat for a month.

11. The hikers who are venturing down into the canyon must have the necessary supplies if (you, they) hope to be safe.

12. Mason and Morgan made a thank you card for (them, their) babysitter at the end of the summer.

13. Mom treated (herself, itself) to a day at the spa with (she, her) best friend.

14. My dog and (me, I) are going to pack some treats before (we, they) head to the park.

15. Each of the boys (handle, handles) the fragile fossil carefully.

16. When your friends arrive, tell (them, her) to park in the street.

17. Shane (itself, himself) will be thanking his teachers at the end of the year.

Identify the underlined pronoun in each sentence as a subject pronoun (SP), object pronoun (OP), possessive pronoun (PP), or indefinite pronoun (IP).

18. ________ A tree fell on <u>our</u> shed during the wind storm.

19. ________ Does <u>anyone</u> care that our washing machine is broken?

20. ________ <u>They</u> are coming over for dinner around 6:00.

21. ________ Quan asked <u>them</u> to wait their turn.

22. ________ Reba loves <u>your</u> new sweatshirt.

23. ________ My mom asked me to do <u>something</u>, but I can't remember what it was.

24. ________ I am going to the dentist because <u>my</u> tooth aches.

Name ______________________________

Lesson 1.10 Action Verbs

Action verbs tell the action of the sentence. The action can be physical or mental.

Rufus **jumped** off the dock to catch the ball. (physical action)
We **hope** to arrive on time. (mental action)
Straighten the books on the shelf, please. (physical action)
Horace **feels** sick today. (mental action)

Action verbs may also be in past, present, or future tense.

Arianna **checked** her email before class. (past)
Arianna **checks** her email before class. (present)
Arianna **will check** her email before class. (future)

Complete each sentence with an action verb. There may be more than one correct answer, but the action verb you choose should make sense in the sentence.

1. The star ______________________ brightly in the night sky.

2. My father ______________________ we were leaving today, but it's actually tomorrow.

3. Tomorrow morning, I ______________________ bags of cans from friends to return to the store.

4. The circus ______________________ to town next month.

5. Rylee ______________________ a short story that she shared with the class.

6. Crew ______________________ the rumble of thunder off in the distance.

7. I ______________________ play dough, vinegar, baking soda, and newspaper for my experiment.

8. The cardinal ______________________ a nest in our hanging basket.

Name ______________________________

Lesson 1.10 Action Verbs

Read each sentence below. Underline action verbs that describe a physical action. Circle action verbs that describe a mental action.

1. In school this week we are learning about the people of Iceland.

2. People who live in Iceland are called Icelanders.

3. Almost the entire population of Iceland can read and write.

4. Icelanders enjoy great medical care, good education, and high incomes.

5. Because the living conditions are so good, Icelanders can expect to live long lives.

6. Most Icelanders share a similar look of blond hair and blue eyes.

7. Icelanders read more than people of any other country.

8. Fish and lamb are enjoyed by most Icelanders.

9. Icelanders know they can be proud of their culture.

10. I hope to visit Iceland someday.

Can you choose two of the action verbs below to include in two sentences? Try it.

achieved **change** **inspired** **will provide** **remembered**

1. ______________________________

2. ______________________________

Name ______________________________________

Lesson 1.11 Subject-Verb Agreement

Subject-verb agreement means that the verb must agree in number with the subject of the sentence. If the subject is singular, use a singular verb. If the subject is plural, use a plural verb.

The **owl hunts** from the tree. The **owls hunt** from the tree.

When a sentence contains a compound subject connected by the word **and,** use a plural verb.

Pete and Finn go to doggy daycare together.

When a sentence contains a compound subject connected by the words **or** or **nor**, use a verb that agrees with the subject that is closer to the verb.

Neither the teacher **nor** her **students think** the bus is going to leave on time.

Either the girls **or Sammy orders** a salad.

If the subject and the verb are separated by a word or words, be sure that the verb still agrees with the subject.

Her **shirt**, as well as her shoes, **is** ruined.

Complete each sentence below with the correct form of the verb in parentheses.

1. Tony ______________________ marathons all year long. (run)
2. He ______________________ all around the world to compete. (travel)
3. Neither the travel nor the marathons ______________________ him out. (tire)
4. His friends and family ______________________ him on from home. (cheer)
5. They ______________________ supporting him. (like)
6. Tony ______________________ for a running shoe company. (work)
7. His clothes, as well as his shoes, ______________________ the company logo on them. (has)
8. Tony ______________________ the shoes he sells, so he can tell people how they fit. (wear)

Name ______________________________

Lesson 1.11 Subject-Verb Agreement

The following sentences have errors in subject-verb agreement. Rewrite each sentence with correct subject-verb agreement. Underline the new verbs you used.

1. Tasha and her friends is going camping.

____

2. Tasha spend all morning cleaning the camper to get it ready.

____

3. She vacuum the floors and wipes the counters.

____

4. An hour before they leave, Natalia and Shay comes over.

____

5. They packs their overnight bags in the back of Tasha's car.

____

6. Then Seth arrive and tosses his pillow and sleeping bag into the car.

____

7. He squeeze his guitar against the roof of the car.

____

8. Tasha close the trunk and they drove away.

____

Explain what it means for a subject and verb to agree.

____

Name ______________________________

Lesson 1.12 Transitive and Intransitive Verbs

Transitive verbs are action verbs that are incomplete without a direct object.

Ross **picked** some blueberries.

Ross picked is not a complete sentence. The transitive verb **picked** needs a direct object (some blueberries) to complete the sentence.

Nellie **tossed** the trash into the dumpster.

In this sentence, the transitive verb **tossed** needs a direct object (the trash) to complete the sentence.

Intransitive verbs are action verbs that do not have to have a direct object.

The dogs **ran** into the lake.

Read each sentence below. Underline transitive verbs once and intransitive verbs twice. For each transitive verb, circle the direct object.

1. The airplane rumbled loudly as it flew overhead.
2. Neyla tasted the sauce in the red squirt bottle.
3. Kody voted in the last election.
4. Miguel told me a joke that wasn't funny.
5. Edwardo remained in the hospital overnight after his surgery.
6. Oscar painted a scene on his new canvas.

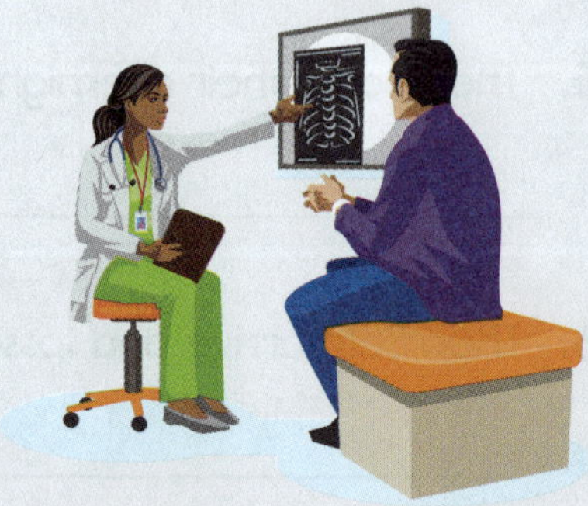

Can you write one sentence with a transitive verb and one sentence with an intransitive verb? Try it!

transitive verb

1. ______________________________

intransitive verb

2. ______________________________

Name ______________________________

Lesson 1.12 Transitive and Intransitive Verbs

The verb in each sentence below is in bold. On the line, write **T** if it is a transitive verb and **I** if it is an intransitive verb. Then, rewrite the sentence using the verb in the opposite way.

Example: I Tia **eats** dinner at 7:00 every night.
Tia eats quickly if she has basketball practice.

1. ________ Caitlyn **walks** up and down the beach looking for dolphins.

____

2. ________ The puppies **played** fetch at the park all afternoon.

____

3. ________ Even though she's taken just one class, Bella **sculpts** artfully.

____

4. ________ The birds **bathed** playfully in the overflowing birdbath.

____

5. ________ The smell of the rotten eggs **spoiled** the picnic.

____

6. ________ Neil **studied** every night for a week for his final exam.

____

Write a sentence for each of these verbs.

Transitive verbs: drive, rake
Intransitive verbs: arrive, smirk

7. ______________________________

8. ______________________________

9. ______________________________

10. ______________________________

Name ______________________________

Lesson 1.13 Helping and Linking Verbs

Helping verbs help form the main verb in a sentence. Forms of the verbs **be, have,** and **do** are the most common helping verbs.

I **have started** riding five miles on my bike.

Hailey **is planning** to paint her bedroom light purple.

Other helping verbs are **can, could, will, would, may, might, shall, should,** and **must.**

Linking verbs connect a subject to a noun or adjective. They do not express an action. The most common linking verbs are forms of the verb **to be**, such as **is, are, was, were, been,** and **am.**

I **am** sad that I missed seeing my grandma! The birds **were** fighting over a worm.

Other common linking verbs relate to the five senses (**smell, look, taste, feel, sound**) or a state of being (**appear, seem, become, grow, remain**).

The cheese in the refrigerator **smells** funny! That car **appears** to turn purple in the sunlight.

In each sentence below, underline the verb. On the line, write **LV** or **HV** to identify it as a linking verb or helping verb.

1. ________ Claude Monet was a famous Impressionist painter.

2. ________ Monet had founded Impressionism with other artists.

3. ________ Many of Monet's paintings seem to be inspired by water.

4. ________ At 15 years old, Monet had become known for his caricatures, or drawings of people.

5. ________ At 20 years old, Monet was drafted into the military in Algeria.

6. ________ None of his artwork from Algeria seems to have survived his time there.

7. ________ Monet had struggled financially early in life, but he found success as he got older.

8. ________ Many of Monet's paintings have sold for millions of dollars apiece.

Name ______________________________

Lesson 1.13 Helping and Linking Verbs

Read the selection below. Underline a linking verb or helping verb to complete the sentences.

Food (is, are) a part of culture. People all around the world eat foods that reflect their culture and traditions. Some foods might (seem, remain) different or strange to people who are not part of that culture, but they are very normal. Some cultures use food to celebrate events or holidays. In China, people (will, should) share a whole steamed fish to celebrate the Chinese New Year. In Mexico, people (can, has) eat Bread of the Dead to celebrate The Day of the Dead. In Turkey, the entire village (was, will) make a stew to celebrate a wedding. Some cultures use food to honor their religions too. People (will, had) fast, or not eat, for days to show commitment to their religion.

You (should, may) be surprised to learn that not every culture celebrates birthdays with a cake. Many cultures (has, have) a different way of celebrating. People in the Netherlands eat birthday pancakes. Russians celebrate with a fruit pie. In South Korea, people (will, were) eat seaweed soup on their birthday. In Ghana, which (is, are) in West Africa, people celebrate their birthday with a breakfast dish of eggs and yams. It (appears, becomes) that there (is, are) many ways to say "Happy Birthday" around the globe. Maybe you (will, did) want to try one of these other foods for your next birthday.

Can you think of an interesting food you have tried? Write a few sentences about it. Underline linking verbs and circle helping verbs in your sentences.

____

____

____

Name ______________________________

Lesson 1.14 Gerunds, Participles, and Infinitives

Gerunds, **participles**, and **infinitives** are other kinds of verbs. These verbs take the role of another part of speech in some circumstances.

A **gerund** is a verb that is used as a noun. A verb can take the form of the noun when the ending *-ing* is added.

Biking is a great way to get outside and enjoy warm weather.
(The subject **biking** is a noun in the sentence)

A **participle** is a verb that is used as an adjective. A verb can take the form of an adjective when the endings **-ing** or **-ed** are added.

The **crying** baby could not fall asleep. (**crying** *modifies* **baby**)
The **wrecked** car could not be repaired. (**wrecked** *modifies* **car**)

An **infinitive** is a verb that is used as a noun, adjective, or adverb. A verb can take the form of a noun, adjective, or adverb when preceded by the word **to**.

To read on a rainy day is relaxing.
(The verb **to read** acts as the subject, or noun, of the sentence.)
The quickest way **to travel** is by airplane.
(The verb **to travel** acts as an adjective modifying **way**.)
Lydia had a suggestion **to offer**.
(The verb **to offer** acts as an adverb modifying **suggestion**.)

Complete each sentence with word(s) from the box. Then, identify the word(s) you wrote with a **G** for gerund, a **P** for participle, or an I for infinitive.

to swim	**hanging**	**to write**	**wagging**	**to say**	**growing**

1. ______________ a poem that rhymes is not easy. ________

2. The ______________ tail on the excited dog was hitting the wall. ________

3. My cousins like ______________ in the lake when they visit us. ________

4. The mayor had a lot ______________ when he got to the podium. ________

5. ______________ vegetables in a garden makes it easy to have fresh veggies all summer long. ________

6. Our ______________ basket always attracts hummingbirds. ________

Name ______________________________

Lesson 1.14 Gerunds, Participles, and Infinitives

Each sentence has either a gerund, participle, or infinitive. Circle the word and then write what type of word it is on the line.

1. Hiking with my dog is my favorite hobby.

   ____

2. There are hiking trails in the dunes near us.

   ____

3. Once I had to run because bees were chasing us.

   ____

4. Swimming in the lake is my dog's favorite part of our hike.

   ____

5. It is good for his legs to swim every day.

   ____

6. He likes swimming on hot, summer days.

   ____

Can you think of a verb? Use it in three different ways: as a gerund, participle, and infinitive. Write your sentences on the lines.

____

____

____

Name ______________________

Lesson 1.15 Verb Tenses

A **present tense** verb describes an action that is happening now or happens regularly.
We **watch** the owl swoop down to catch its prey.

A **present tense** verb can also express a generalization or fact.
The Bill of Rights **guarantees** each citizen will have certain freedoms.

A **past tense** verb describes an action that happened in the past. For many verbs, the past tense is formed by adding **-ed** to the base form of the verb.
The kids **studied** into the evening for the final exam.

For some verbs, the past tense is a different word.
Construction **began** last week on the new community pool. (past tense of **begin**)

A **future tense** verb describes a future action. The word **will** is used before the verb.
The students **will arrive** in London tomorrow evening.

Rewrite each sentence using the indicated tense.

1. Cheers filled the theater as the movie ended.

   Present tense: ______________________

2. Historical fiction novels line the bookshelves in our living room.

   Future tense: ______________________

3. Painting supplies will be delivered to the classroom today.

   Past tense: ______________________

4. The woodpecker pecked at the tree trunk to find bugs.

   Present tense: ______________________

5. The photograph looks amazing in that new frame!

   Future tense: ______________________

Name ______________________________

Lesson 1.15 Verb Tenses

Proofread the following paragraph. Use the proofreading marks to correct mistakes with verb tenses and irregular verbs. Insert the correctly spelled words.

delete	insert

Yesterday, our class will visit an outdoor wildlife center. After we all taked our seats in the main lobby, the director, Mr. Langford, will welcome us and told us about what we'd be doing during our visit. He introduced us to some reptiles, amphibians, and birds of prey that we could possibly saw as we took our tour on the many acres of open land.

While walking near ponds and down trails, we keeped our eyes open for signs of life. We each had a notebook in which to keep notes about what we seen, including bugs, frogs, salamanders, snakes, owls, eagles, certain flowers and plants, and more. Each group leader will have a net they could use to carefully scooped up small creatures if we spotted some. This will allow us to examine them more closely before putting them back into their habitat. Once back at the learning center, we all will share what we founded and learned during our outdoor adventure.

Before we leaved to go back to school, Mr. Langford will tell us about the mission of the outdoor wildlife center. It raises money and awareness about outdoor education and conservation. The program hoped to help protect and restores natural habitats.

Name ______________________________

Lesson 1.16 Verb Tenses: Progressive

Progressive verb tenses describe ongoing, or continuing, actions.

A **present progressive** verb describes an action or condition that is ongoing in the present. A present progressive verb is made up of the present tense of the helping verb **be** and the present participle of the main verb.

The stew **is cooking** in the slow cooker. The bees **are buzzing** in their hive.

A **past progressive** verb describes an action or condition that was ongoing at some time in the past. A past progressive verb is made up of the past form of the helping verb **be** and the present participle of the main verb.

Laticia **was dancing** in her room to her favorite song.
The babies **were crying** during the storm.

Underline the progressive verbs in each sentence. Then, write **past** or **present** on the line to identify the progressive verb tense.

1. Asia is drinking orange juice with her breakfast. ____________
2. Weeds are growing all over our backyard. ____________
3. Citizens were willing to speak up against the injustice. ____________
4. My neighbor is washing his patio furniture. ____________
5. I was photographing birds when it started to rain. ____________
6. The students were listening quietly to the author speak about his book. ____________
7. Two owls are hooting at dusk in the woods behind our house. ____________

8. Adrian is mashing potatoes to help his parents with dinner. ____________

Name ____________________

Lesson 1.16 Verb Tenses: Progressive

Use the past progressive forms of the verbs below to complete the paragraph.

bite	grab	hang	hiss	ignore	laugh
paw	pout	squeak	taunt	try	work

Ms. Amendo had a dog named Buster. One day while trying to work from home, Buster ____________ to distract her so she would play with him. Every chance he could get he ____________ his toy behind her chair. She ____________ him the best she could, but he ____________ his toy harder and harder so it would squeak louder. She finally turned around to scold him, but within seconds she ____________ because he had bitten the toy so hard, all the stuffing had exploded out of it. Buster had his head resting on the toy and ____________ because he had ruined it. Now Ms. Amendo could get some work done.

But just when she thought all was quiet, Ms. Amendo heard hissing. Buster had found the cat, Whiskers, and was now bothering her. Whiskers ____________ at Buster from high up on the back of a chair. Buster ____________ Whiskers by nipping at the end of her tail that ____________ down from the chair. Whiskers ____________ at Buster's head while hissing and looking very annoyed. Did that stop Buster? Nope! While Whiskers was trying to tell Buster to leave her alone, Buster lunged at Whiskers and Whiskers sprung from the chair to the curtain. She ____________ onto it with her sharp claws. The curtain and the rod came crashing down to the floor, and Whiskers sprung underneath the couch for protection. With all the commotion, Ms. Amendo ____________ from home, but not getting much done.

Name ___________________________________

Lesson 1.17 Verb Tenses: Perfect

Verb tenses tell when in time something happened—in the past, currently, or in the future.

The **past perfect** shows that an action was completed before another action in the past. It is formed with the verb **had** and a past participle.

The sloth **had climbed** the tree so it could hang upside down.

The **present perfect** shows that something happened in the past. The action may still be going on. The present perfect is formed with the present tense of the verb **have** (**have** or **has**) and a past participle.

Chang **has baked** an apple pie twice before today.

The **future perfect** shows that an action will be completed before a future time or a future action. It is formed with the words **will have** and a past participle.

By Friday, we **will have read** the first four chapters in our book.

Read each sentence below. The perfect tense verb appears in bold. On the line, write **PP** if it is in past perfect, **PRP** if it is present perfect, or **FP** if it is in future perfect.

1. ________ Bianca Rodriguez and her family **have attended** the Logan County Fair every year since they moved to Indiana.
2. ________ My dog, Ruby, **had rolled** in the mud before coming inside.
3. ________ Meah **will have worked** 24 hours already this week.
4. ________ The mail person **had delivered** our mail in a snowstorm.
5. ________ Nathan **will have flown** from New York to Hawaii in one day.
6. ________ Lydia **will have worked** at the ice cream shop all summer.

Name ______________________________

Lesson 1.17 Verb Tenses: Perfect

Read each sentence. On the line, write the bold verb in the past, present, or future perfect tense. The words in parentheses will tell you which tense to use.

1. The boys **ask** ____________________ a group of kids to join their basketball game. (present perfect)

2. Officer Reyez **talk** ____________________ to our school about safety. (past perfect)

3. By the end of today, Lucia **bake** ____________________ enough cookies for the bake sale. (future perfect)

4. Hugo **earn** ____________________ enough money from shoveling driveways to buy new shoes. (past perfect)

5. My family **live** ____________________ in our house since I was born. (present perfect)

6. Eli **finish** ____________________ power washing the deck by noon. (past perfect)

7. By next summer, the city **built** ____________________ the new sports complex. (future perfect)

8. Hannah **wash** ____________________ the dishes while her mom went for a walk. (past perfect)

Can you write two sentences about activities or hobbies that interest you? Try it. Choose two verb tenses from above to use in your sentences.

____

____

Name ______________________________

Review Lessons 1.10–1.17

Circle the type of verb indicated in parentheses.

1. Holly swam the entire length of the pool four times. (action verb)
2. Elijah was excited to go to the library. (helping verb)
3. The old house on the corner feels spooky to me. (linking verb)
4. LaToya called the store to ask if they are hiring. (action verb)
5. Mom has told you to clean your room twice. (helping verb)
6. The raft drifted down the slow-moving river. (action verb)
7. The muffins Janese made taste fantastic! (linking verb)
8. Pho rode her bike to the pet store to look at fish. (action verb)

In the sentences below, circle the transitive verbs and underline the intransitive verbs.

9. Liv passed the broccoli to her little brother.
10. Lee rode his scooter to the splash pad with his babysitter.
11. The cat hissed loudly at the dog.
12. The girls painted pictures for their grandparents.

Complete each sentence below with the correct form of the verb in parentheses.

13. The flag ______________________ in the stiff breeze. (wave)
14. The church bell ______________________ at noon. (clang)
15. Cats, dogs, and fish ______________________ perfect pets. (make)
16. Neither wolves nor other large predators ______________________ welcome near a farm. (to be)

Name ________________________________

Review Lessons 1.10–1.17

Identify the underlined word using the key in the box. Write your answer on the line.

a. gerund	b. participle	c. infinitive

17. ______ Ever since he was a puppy, swimming has been Rex's favorite activity.

18. ______ The screaming child was carried out of the grocery store by her mother.

19. ______ The soaring hawk glided above the trees.

20. ______ In order to enjoy a concert, it helps to know some of the songs.

21. ______ Listening closely to directions is very important.

22. ______ Ethan tried to hit the golf ball as straight as possible.

Rewrite each sentence below in the tense indicated in parentheses.

23. (present progressive) The children sleep in the loft.

____

24. (past progressive) Dolphins follow the tourist boats.

____

25. (past progressive) When her friends came over, Lucy eats lunch.

____

26. (present progressive) Ally visits her aunt and uncle next month.

____

Name ______________________________

Lesson 1.18 Adjectives and Predicate Adjectives

An **adjective** is a word that describes a noun or pronoun. It offers more information about the word it modifies. Adjectives often come before the noun or pronoun they describe. They answer the question **What kind? How many?** or **Which one?**

The **dark** clouds opened up and dropped **heavy** rain.

The **ripe** avocado made the **tropical** salad even more delicious.

Proper adjectives are capitalized.

Onion rings came with the **French** dip sandwich.

The **Ukrainian** president was interviewed many times this week.

A **predicate adjective** follows a linking verb (a form of the verb **to be, smell, look, taste, feel, sound, appear, seem, become, grow,** or **remain**). A predicate adjective modifies the subject of a sentence.

The shoes look **expensive**.

Underline each common or proper adjective you find. Circle the predicate adjectives.

1. The crunchy chips were a perfect choice with my Caesar salad.

2. Easter eggs are usually dyed in pastel colors.

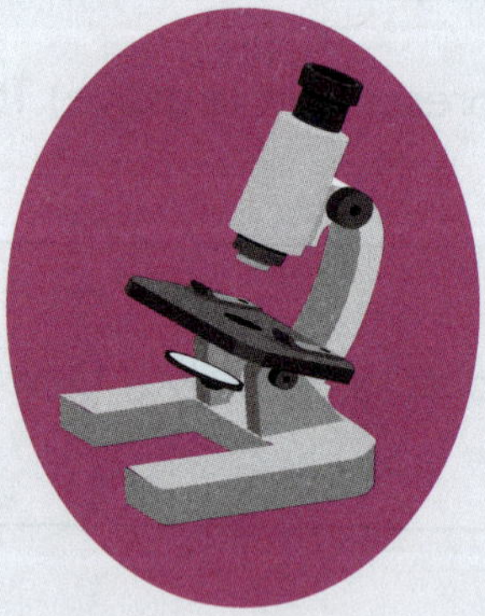

3. The molecules appeared large through the microscope.

4. Alexander grew weary as midnight approached.

5. Alaskan salmon is a very healthy fish to eat.

6. The air smelled smoky and looked hazy.

7. At the busy beach, I ran through the hot sand to get to the cool water.

8. My mom and I took Italian cooking classes at the community center.

Name ______________________________

Lesson 1.18 Adjectives and Predicate Adjectives

Fill in the blanks with adjectives. When you are done, circle all the predicate adjectives you used. There is more than one correct answer for each item.

1. I felt ____________ when the ____________ licorice got stuck in my teeth.
2. After the skunk sprayed, our house smelled ____________.
3. My mom became ____________ when our neighbor threw trash in our yard.
4. Terence sat on the ____________ couch and covered himself with a ____________ blanket.
5. Ruby felt ____________ as she opened her email to find her acceptance letter.
6. My ____________ feet hurt so bad after hiking the ____________ mountain.
7. My dad thought the heavy metal music sounded ____________.
8. The ____________ bread smelled ____________ as it baked in the oven.
9. The dog grew ____________ as the ____________ boat rolled over the ____________ waves.

10. My dad and I decorated the tree with ____________ bulbs, ____________ ornaments, and a ____________ star on top.

Can you describe a beautiful or unusual place you've visited? Try it. Use at least five adjectives.

____

____

____

____

Name ______________________________

Lesson 1.19 Comparative and Superlative Adjectives

Comparative adjectives compare two nouns, and **superlative adjectives** compare three or more nouns.

big, bigger, biggest **smart, smarter, smartest** **pretty, prettier, prettiest**

For adjectives that end in **y**, change the **y** to **i** before adding the suffixes **-er** or **-est**.

Comparing two nouns:
My dog's new bed is **softer** than his old one.

Comparing three or more nouns:
Rippin' Rider is the **scariest** roller coaster.

Comparative and superlative adjectives can also be formed by adding the words **more** (comparative) and **most** (superlative) before the adjective. Use **more** and **most** with adjectives that have two or more syllables.
That is the **most beautiful** church! Caleb is **more rambunctious** today.

Draw a line to match the adjectives in Column B to their sentences in Column A.

Column A	Column B
1. Please take the ____________ way home because I'm late.	busiest
2. The weather today is supposed to be ____________ than it was yesterday.	driest
3. The Atacama Desert in Chile is the ____________ place on earth.	windier
4. LaGuardia Airport is the ____________ airport I've ever been in.	prettier
5. Maya's joke is the ____________ one I've ever heard!	fastest
6. Mr. Stein's tests are more ____________ than Mr. Phipp's tests.	dangerous
7. Our garden is ____________ this year since we've added pink rose bushes.	funniest
8. One of the most ____________ things I've ever done is skydive.	difficult

Name ______________________________

Lesson 1.19 Comparative and Superlative Adjectives

Write the correct form of the adjective in parentheses to complete each sentence below.

1. Our new neighbors upstairs are ______________ than the people who used to live there. (comparative of **noisy**)

2. My uncle became ______________ as the boat kept rocking back and forth. (comparative of **sick**)

3. The ______________ ocean temperature ever recorded was 132.8° in the Red Sea. (superlative of **hot**)

4. My dog won "______________ Costume" at the fair for being dressed up as a chicken. (superlative of **silly**)

5. Lake Superior is ______________ than Lake Michigan. (comparative of **deep**)

6. Brown hair and brown eyes is the ______________ combination in the world. (superlative of **common**)

7. In a storm, hail is ______________ than rain. (comparative of **damaging**)

8. The shelter hired Justin because he seemed ______________ than the other people they interviewed. (comparative of **compassionate**)

Can you write a sentence for each item below? Try it.

1. Use the comparative of **frustrating**.

____

2. Use the superlative of **simple**.

____

Name ___________________________________

Lesson 1.20 Adverbs and Intensifiers

Adverbs modify, or describe, verbs. An adverb tells **how, when**, or **where** an action occurs.

The crowd cheered **wildly**. (tells **how** the crowd cheered)

Our airplane was **late**. (tells **when** it arrived)

Matty threw the ball **over** the fence. (tells **where** Matty threw the ball)

Adverbs can also modify adjectives or other adverbs.

The afternoon was **horribly stormy**. (**horribly** modifies the adjective **stormy**)

My big brother got home **relatively late** last night. (**relatively** modifies the adverb **late**)

Many, but not all, adverbs are formed by adding **-ly** to adjectives.

Intensifiers are adverbs that add emphasis or intensity to adjectives or other adverbs.

This word bank shows commonly used intensifiers.

almost	**extremely**	**just**	**nearly**	**practically**	**quite**	**rather**
really	**so**	**somewhat**	**such**	**too**	**very**	

The West Coast is **extremely hot** this summer. The boy ran into the street **quite recklessly**.

Circle the adverb(s) or intensifier in each sentence. Underline the word that is being modified.

1. The mountain roads were extremely curvy.
2. The raspberries were rather fragile, so we picked them gently.
3. The student nervously raised her hand to answer the question.
4. Tubing behind a boat is really fun on a hot, summer day.

5. Willy's tennis ball rolled under the couch.
6. The large box was too heavy for the delivery person to pick up.

Name ____

Lesson 1.20 Adverbs and Intensifiers

Fill in each blank with an adverb or intensifier. Use the words shown in the box, either to fill in the blanks or for ideas. Be sure the words make sense where you place them in the sentences.

too	very	practically	politely	freshly	carefully
lately	quite	initially	mostly	generously	grumpily
originally	outside	desperately	quickly	icily	obviously
only	barely	much	so	reluctantly	gently
especially	profusely	such	helpfully	truly	
eagerly	loudly				

________________ early Tuesday morning, Travis's alarm rang ________________. The noise startled him from a ________________ deep sleep. He was ________________ annoyed, but then he ________________ remembered why he had to wake ________________ early. Today, Travis would begin ________________ volunteering at the local food pantry. The pantry ________________ provided meals for those in need. The breakfast shift was ________________ important. A child could get a ________________ made breakfast before heading to school. Travis ________________ dressed and rushed ________________ down the stairs. The sun ________________ peaked above the horizon, so the sky was ________________ still dark. Travis had ________________ planned to bike to the pantry, because it was not ________________ far from his apartment. Then, he looked ________________ at the thermometer hanging ________________ near the window. The temperature was ________________ cold at just 30°! Travis ________________ shivered at the thought of riding in ________________ freezing weather. Instead, he trudged ________________ back up the stairs and tapped ________________ at his ________________ older brother's door. He heard Aaron ________________ ask, "What?" But when he ________________ explained why he ________________ needed a ride, he jumped ________________ out of bed. He was ________________ impressed with Travis and ________________ willing to help. It took ________________ a few minutes to drive to the pantry. Travis thanked his brother before heading into the building, a huge grin ________________ spreading across his face.

Name ______________________________

Lesson 1.21 Comparative and Superlative Adverbs

Like comparative adjectives, **comparative adverbs** compare two actions.

Our soccer team played **more skillfully** than their team.

Owen got home **later** than Hunter.

Superlative adverbs compare three or more actions.

The Troost's house is the **most beautifully** decorated house in town.

My school bus is always the **latest**.

Short adverbs are formed using **-er** for comparatives and **-est** for superlatives. Long adverbs use the words **more** and *most*, or for negative comparisons, *less* or **least**.

The sun rose **earlier** this morning than it did yesterday.

The sun rises **earliest** on Cadillac Mountain in Maine.

Jamie jumped into the camper **more enthusiastically** than her brother did.

Ben jumped into the camper **least enthusiastically** of his whole family.

Rewrite each sentence below using a comparative or superlative adverb.

1. Clare stared seriously at the treasure map.

   comparative: ______________________________

2. The mouse scurried quietly across the garage floor.

   superlative: ______________________________

3. The International Space Station will be visible soon.

   comparative: ______________________________

4. The service at Mama Mia's Pizza was reviewed favorably online.

   comparative: ______________________________

5. I am anxiously awaiting my first violin lesson.

   superlative: ______________________________

6. Chao yelled enthusiastically when it was his turn to get on the ride.

   superlative: ______________________________

Name ____

Lesson 1.21 Comparative and Superlative Adverbs

Complete each sentence with the correct form of the adverb in parentheses.

1. Hans reacted ____________________ to the roller coasters than the waterpark. (excitedly)
2. Alex counted his money ____________________ than his sister did. (carefully)
3. The petite mutt barks ____________________ than the large Labrador. (angrily)
4. The A Bus stops ____________________ in the city than the C Bus. (frequently)
5. I painted the landscape ____________________ than my sister did. (skillfully)
6. Lucy talks ____________________ than Charlie. (often)
7. Kai danced ____________________ of all. (gracefully)
8. I took the English final exam ____________________ than everyone else. (early)
9. The package arrived ____________________ than it was supposed to. (late)
10. Of all my plants, the ferns grew the ____________________. (quickly)

Choose four adverbs from the box. For two of them, write sentences using the comparative form. For the other two, write sentences using the superlative form.

quickly	delicately	graciously	affectionately	eagerly
carelessly	sluggishly	often	far	lovingly

11. ____
12. ____
13. ____
14. ____

Name ______________________________

Lesson 1.22 Adjectives and Adverbs

Some adjectives and adverbs are easy to confuse with one another.
Use a **predicate adjective** after a linking verb (forms of the verb **to be** and verbs like **seem, taste, grow,** and **become**).

The music **sounded joyful** as it streamed through the open windows.

Use an **adverb** to describe an action verb.

Zora **played joyfully**, as though a large audience was listening.

In the first example, the adjective **joyful** follows the linking verb **sounded** and modifies the subject **music**. In the second example, the adverb **joyfully** modifies the action verb **played**.

The words **good, bad, well,** and **badly** are often used incorrectly. **Good** and **bad** are adjectives, and **well** and **badly** are adverbs.

Your homemade yogurt **tastes good**.
Bubbles and Ringo **ate well** today, even though they were sick last night.

Complete each sentence with the adjective or adverb that fits. Write the adjective or adverb on the line.

1. Her right turn down Oak Street was ______________ and startled me. sudden

2. The chipmunk darted ______________ across the yard. suddenly

---

3. Levi felt ______________ as he waited for the important phone call. anxiously

4. Annaleese waited ______________ outside the principal's office. anxious

---

5. Jill watched ______________ as the waitress walked out with her cake. excited

6. As the clock ran down, the team grew ______________ about a win. excitedly

---

7. The chef in the baking competition performed ______________. bad

8. Link felt ______________ for dropping the bowl of ice cream on the floor. badly

Name ______________________________

Lesson 1.22 Adjectives and Adverbs

Write **Adj.** or **Adv.** to identify each bold word as an adjective or adverb. If the word is an adjective, underline the linking verb it follows. If it is an adverb, circle the action verb it follows.

1. __________ The pink hydrangeas that Amy brought over looked **stunning**.

2. __________ Stanley barked **incessantly** at the delivery driver.
3. __________ The full moon shone **brightly** in the night sky.
4. __________ The ladder that Mike climbed felt **unstable**, but he used it anyway.
5. __________ Although we were in a rural area, our cell phone reception was **good**.
6. __________ Mikhala thought the raw oysters tasted **gross**.
7. __________ The melody sounded **elegant** as it floated out of the ballroom.
8. __________ RJ did not do **well** on his flute test for first chair.
9. __________ The door opened **completely**, and out stepped a seven-foot man.
10. __________ Olivia made a goal, and her family cheered **wildly** for her.
11. __________ My grandpa grew **confused** as I tried to explain how to sync his phone to his car.
12. __________ I became **concerned** after two hours of Aleisha not texting me back.

Can you write one sentence containing an adverb and one sentence containing an adjective? Try it.

1. ______________________________
2. ______________________________

Name ____________________________________

Lesson 1.23 Prepositions and Prepositional Phrases

Prepositions are words that show the relationship between a noun or pronoun and another word in the sentence.

The skier skied *down* the mountain. The grill is *beside* the railing.

Some common prepositions are *above, across, after, along, at, away, because, before, behind, below, beneath, beside, between, by, down, during, except, for, from, in, into, near, of, off, on, outside, over, to, toward, under, until, up, with, within,* and *without.*

Prepositional phrases include the prepositions and objects (nouns or pronouns) that follow the preposition, and the modifiers of the object. Prepositional phrases tell *when* or *where* something is happening.

The scared raccoon hid *under the deck.* (Where? Under the deck)

My family left on our road trip *before the sun came up.* (When? Before the sun came up)

Complete each sentence with a preposition from the word bank. There may be more than one correct answer for each item.

around	**beneath**	**between**	**during**
from	**on**	**outside**	**over**

1. A large amount of algae was floating ____________________ the surface of the lake.

2. The tornado siren went off ____________________ the lacrosse game.

3. The biker sped ____________________ trees down the dirt trail.

4. We could hardly hear the hot air balloon as it floated ____________________ us.

5. I like to wonder about what lies ____________________ the surface of the ocean.

6. I think my dad drove ____________________ the roundabout too many times.

7. Hail was falling ____________________ the sky as we took shelter in the small building.

8. Ada left her wet rain boots ____________________ so she wouldn't track water in.

Name ____

Lesson 1.23 Prepositions and Prepositional Phrases

Circle each prepositional phrase. Underline each preposition. The number in parentheses will tell you how many prepositions each sentence contains.

1. The *Titanic* was going to sail from Southampton, England, to New York City. (2)

2. The impressive ship was built in Ireland within three years. (2)

3. Over 2,200 people were on board the *Titanic*. (2)

4. In the *Titanic* first class dining room, guests dined on steak with potatoes, oysters, French cheeses, and more. (3)

5. First class passengers had large rooms above the water line with fancy furniture. (2)

6. Third class passengers had rooms by the loud engines at the bottom of the ship. (3)

7. The *Titanic* was carrying mail and packages over to New York City too. (1)

8. Just before midnight, the *Titanic* hit an iceberg beneath the surface of the water. (3)

Can you think of an important news event that has happened lately? Write about it. Underline each preposition you use.

Name ____

Lesson 1.24 Conjunctions

Conjunctions connect individual words or groups of words in sentences.

Coordinate conjunctions connect words, phrases, or independent clauses that are equal or of the same type. Coordinate conjunctions are **and, but, or, nor, for,** and **yet.**

The dog was soft **and** silky after his bath.

Correlative conjunctions come in pairs and are used together.
Both/and, either/or, and **neither/nor** are examples of correlative conjunctions.

Subordinate conjunctions connect dependent clauses to independent clauses in order to complete the meaning. **After, although, as long as, since, unless, whether,** and **while** are examples of subordinate conjunctions.

Write a conjunction from the right column on a line for a sentence it completes on the left.

1. Hailey baked a cake, ____________ I baked a pie.

2. There was a loud crash, ____________ we went outside.

3. Fern fell asleep ____________ she was tired.

4. I don't buy hot lunch ____________ there are chicken tenders.

5. ____________ Jed ____________ Ned could climb the tree.

6. Ahmed didn't know the answer, ____________ he still raised his hand to answer the question.

7. ____________ they're serving chicken or steak doesn't matter to me.

8. ____________ Leesa ____________ Keisha were running for class treasurer.

both/and

because

and

whether

so

neither/nor

yet

unless

Name ______________________________

Lesson 1.24 Conjunctions

Read each phrase. Write them beside the appropriate headings.

the pink and red tulips	**after the wrestling match**
although I couldn't remember his name	**both the concert and the meeting**
either Janelle or Jones	**either in March or April**

Coordinate Conj. ______________________________

____

Correlative Conj. ______________________________

____

Subordinate Conj. ______________________________

____

Write a sentence that includes the item(s) in parentheses.

1. (a subordinate conjunction) ______________________________

____

2. (a correlative conjunction) ______________________________

____

3. (a coordinate conjunction and a subordinate conjunction) ______________________________

____

4. (two coordinate conjunctions) ______________________________

____

Name ______________________________

Lesson 1.25 Interjections

An **interjection** is a word or phrase used to express surprise or strong emotion. Common interjections include:

ah	**alas**	**aw**	**awesome**	**eeek**	**ew**
hey	**hi**	**hurray**	**oh**	**oh, no**	**oops**
ouch	**phew**	**yay**	**yippee**	**yuck**	**wow**

An exclamation mark or a comma is used after an interjection to separate it from the rest of the sentence.

Awesome! I got tickets to the concert! **Ew,** that tomato is rotten!

Begin each sentence with an interjection.

1. ____________________! I stubbed my toe on the couch!

2. ____________________, we probably won't ever have the chance to see this again.

3. ____________________! That was too close!

4. ____________________, those flowers are lovely!

5. ____________________! You're doing such a great job!

6. ____________________, I figured that would happen!

Explain why authors might use interjections in their stories.

____

____

Name ______________________________

Lesson 1.25 Interjections

Each sentence begins with the wrong interjection. Rewrite each sentence with a better interjection.

Common Interjections						
yum	wow	no	hooray	great	hi	oh no
yay	yuck	ha	yes	ouch	oh	

1. Hooray! Are you ok?

____

2. Ouch! That cheese smells bad!

____

3. Yuck! I won the lottery!

____

4. Yum! You are so smart!

____

5. No! My mom said I can go to the mall!

____

6. Ha! I broke my dad's expensive golf club!

____

7. Yes! I failed my math test!

____

8. Hi! That joke is so funny!

____

Can you think of an interjection that you use a lot when you're speaking? Write it down.

____

Name ______________________________

Review Lessons 1.18–1.25

Underline the predicate adjectives. Circle the other adjectives. On the line, write **C** if the adjective is comparative, write **S** if the adjective is superlative, or leave it blank if the adjective is neither comparative nor superlative.

1. ______ The Aztec people were nomadic.

2. ______ Around the year 1300, the Aztecs arrived in what is now central Mexico.

3. ______ They built beautiful temples throughout the region.

4. ______ The temples were large and intricate.

5. ______ The tallest temple was called Templo Mayor.

6. ______ The temples were religious sites.

7. ______ The Aztec people worshipped many gods.

8. ______ Some words we use today sound similar to words the Aztecs used.

9. ______ The Aztec civilization lasted longer than 200 years.

10. ______ Many Aztec descendants still live in Mexico today.

As indicated, rewrite each sentence to change the adverb to a comparative or superlative adverb. If the sentence contains an intensifier, circle the intensifier.

11. The raft raced speedily through the rapids.

Superlative: ______________________________

12. Ms. Simmons was really tired this evening, so she trudged sleepily to her bedroom.

Comparative: ______________________________

Name ______________________________

Review Lessons 1.18–1.25

Circle the correct adjective or adverb to complete the sentence.

13. The orchestra sounded (bad, badly) because they hadn't warmed up.

14. Everyone in the auditorium felt (sad, sadly) after listening to the speaker's story.

15. Nia thinks she did (good, well) on her driving test.

16. Bruno waited (nervously, nervous) for the important phone call.

17. Early in the morning, Raymond could hear the (sweet, sweetly) sound of a mourning dove.

Identify the bold word in each sentence. On the line, write **P** if it is a preposition, **C** if it is a conjunction, or **I** if it is an interjection. For sentences that contain a preposition, also underline the prepositional phrase.

18. ______ **Hey**, come back here!

19. ______ The scared skunk ran **behind** the shed.

20. ______ **As long as** the forecast calls for a dry day, we'll go to the beach.

21. ______ Russ will keep taking the bus **until** his car is fixed.

22. ______ My dog won't eat his dog food, **but** he loves his treats.

23. Write a sentence that contains two prepositional phrases: ______________________________

____

24. Write a sentence that contains a coordinate conjunction: ______________________________

____

25. Write a sentence that contains a correlative conjunction: ______________________________

____

26. Write a sentence that contains a subordinate conjunction: ______________________________

____

Name ______________________________

Review Chapter 1

Answer the following questions.

1. What is the difference between a common noun and a proper noun?

____

2. Write two examples of common nouns and two examples of proper nouns.

Common Nouns	Proper Nouns
______	______
______	______

3. Explain what the problem is in this sentence and how you can fix it. Then rewrite the sentence so it is correct.

Our principal always says that if a student wants to succeed, they must put in the work.

Problem: ______________________________

Correct: ______________________________

____

4. Explain what the problem is in this sentence and how you can fix it. Then rewrite the sentence so it is correct.

The people who lives in our neighborhood asked me to shovel their driveway while they are gone.

Problem: ______________________________

Correct: ______________________________

____

5. Write each verb in present tense, past tense, and future tense.

Present	Past	Future
______	______	will make
do	______	______
______	woke	______
______	______	will begin

Name ______________________________

Review Chapter 1

Underline the adjective in each sentence. On the line, write whether it is a comparative (C), superlative (S), or predicate adjective (P).

6. The most exciting thing happened to me yesterday! ______

7. The casserole in the oven smells burned. ______

8. As Tasha's story kept unfolding, my dad grew angrier. ______

9. This summer is definitely hotter than last summer. ______

10. The repair for the car was more expensive than my mom hoped it would be. ______

For each sentence, underline the adverb. Then write on the line whether it tells how, when, or where about the word it modifies. Circle the one intensifier.

11. We gently climbed up the old, rickety ladder. ______________

12. Misha lost her sweatshirt at the game yesterday. ______________

13. Nikea went into the job interview quite confidently. ______________

Underline the prepositional phrases. Circle the conjunctions.

14. The ants climbed up the hill, but they didn't go in the anthill.

15. Since you have a baseball game tonight, let's eat a quick sandwich in the car.

16. Both the dog and its owner were stuck in the downpour.

17. While they were visiting Mexico, Justin and Jana went to the Mayan ruins.

18. I went jogging in the sweltering heat, yet I didn't get very sweaty.

Chapter 2: Sentences

Students will learn about sentences in Chapter 2. First, four different types of sentences are introduced—declarative, imperative, interrogative, and exclamatory.

While declarative and imperative sentences look quite similar, students will be asked to differentiate between the two. Does a sentence give information, or does it give a command or request? They both end with periods, so students will need to determine the intent of the sentence to figure out which type it is.

Interrogative sentences are used to question something or someone, while exclamatory sentences are used to express sudden or strong emotions.

Chapter 2 then moves on to simple, compound, and complex sentences. Students are given practice in determining if sentences are simple or complex based on how many subjects and predicates they have. Students will also look for independent and dependent clauses, as well as subordinate conjunctions or relative pronouns, in helping them determine if sentences are complex. Students will use their creativity to write their own simple, compound, and complex sentences, which often gives students a feeling of ownership and pride.

Lastly, Chapter 2 touches on adjective and adverb clauses, which add more information and detail to writing. Students will work on identifying and writing these clauses so that they will become comfortable with including them in their own writing.

Skills Checklist

- [ ] Identifying and writing declarative, imperative, interrogative, and exclamatory sentences
- [ ] Identifying and writing simple, compound, and complex sentences
- [ ] Identifying and writing adjective and adverb clauses

Helpful Definitions

declarative sentence: a sentence that makes a statement; ends with a period; Example: *I have two dogs.*

interrogative sentence: a sentence that asks a question; ends with a question mark; Example: *Is it supposed to snow today?*

imperative sentence: a sentence that demands that an action be performed; ends with a period or an exclamation mark; Example: *Close the door.*

exclamatory sentence: a sentence that shows emotion; ends with an exclamation mark; Example: *I love it!*

dependent clause: does not present a complete thought, cannot stand alone; Example: *because I was hungry*

independent clause: presents a complete thought, can stand alone as a sentence; Example: *I ate pizza because I was hungry.*

simple sentence: a sentence with one independent clause; Example: *The soup was delicious.*

compound sentence: a sentence with two or more simple sentences; Example: *I was cold, so I grabbed a blanket.*

complex sentence: has one independent clause and one or more dependent clauses; Example: *When the timer goes off, the cookies are done.*

adjective clause: dependent clause that modifies a noun or pronoun and usually follows the word it modifies; Example: *The coat that I bought online is too small.*

adverb clause: dependent clause that modifies a verb, adjective, or adverb; answers *How? When? Where? Why?* or *Under what condition?*; Example: *Once it stops storming, we'll go outside.*

Name ______________________________

Lesson 2.1 Sentence Types

A **declarative sentence** makes a statement about a person, place, thing, or idea and it ends with a period.

A typical hurricane is about 300 miles wide.

An **interrogative sentence** asks a question and ends with a question mark.

What weather conditions cause hurricanes?

An **exclamatory sentence** shows emotion and ends with an exclamation mark.

Wow, look how tall this building is!

An **imperative sentence** demands that an action be performed. The subject of an imperative sentence is usually not expressed, but the subject is normally understood as **you**. Imperative sentences can be punctuated with a period or an exclamation mark.

Board up the windows! Look at the buckets of rain blowing sideways.

Rewrite each sentence as the sentence type indicated.

1. The weather in the eye of a hurricane is calm.

Interrogative: ______________________________

2. The eye of a hurricane can span 20–40 miles wide.

Exclamatory: ______________________________

3. Can you tell me a little bit about hurricanes?

Imperative: ______________________________

4. Is a category 2 hurricane dangerous?

Declarative: ______________________________

5. Are major hurricanes ones with winds over 110mph?

Declarative: ______________________________

6. Ocean temperatures need to be above 79°F for a hurricane to form.

Interrogative: ______________________________

Name ______________________________

Lesson 2.1 Sentence Types

On the line, identify the sentence type as **D** for declarative, **IM** for imperative, **IN** for interrogative, or **E** for exclamatory.

Look up at the sky. ______ What do you see? ______ Are white, puffy clouds floating by? ______ Is it a clear, blue day? ______ Or is it dark and stormy? ______ The sky is often described by writers with fun, descriptive words. ______ Scientists are more precise and scientific with their descriptions. ______ British chemist and lover of clouds Luke Howard created a system for describing clouds based on their appearances in the early 1800s. ______ He classified clouds into three categories: cirrus, stratus, and cumulus. ______ Have you ever seen delicate, wispy clouds? ______ Those are cirrus clouds, and they form more than 20,000 feet above the ground. ______ That's way up there! ______

Stratus clouds are lower in the sky. ______ Their altitude is between 6,000 and 20,000 feet. ______ Guess what stratus clouds look like. ______ Would you like a hint? ______ Drizzle or light snow often falls from stratus clouds. ______ That's right, stratus clouds appear as an overcast sky. ______ It will look like a smooth ceiling of gray or white has covered the sky. ______

Can you guess what most people's favorite clouds are? ______ They're the big, puffy ones. ______ They are called cumulus clouds. ______ Surprisingly, they aren't filled with water. ______ But they can quickly fill with water on a hot, humid day. ______ When this happens, they become cumulonimbus clouds. ______ The sky will darken and you will need to take cover! ______ These are also called thunderheads. ______ Can you guess how they get their name? ______ You're right! ______ They bring thunder, lightning, and heavy rain as they roll in. ______

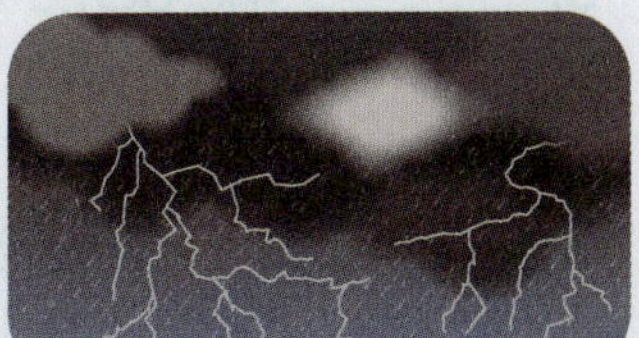

Can you write sentences using two of the four sentence types? Try it!

____

____

Name ____

Lesson 2.2 Simple and Compound Sentences

An **independent clause** presents a complete thought and can stand alone as a sentence.

Simple sentences are sentences with one independent clause. Simple sentences can have one or more subjects and one or more predicates.

The **actors walked** out onto the stage. (one subject, one predicate)

The **actors** and the **directors walked** out onto the stage. (two subjects, one predicate)

The **actors** and the **directors walked** *out onto the stage* and **took** *a bow.* (two subjects, two predicates)

Compound sentences are sentences with two or more simple sentences, or independent clauses. A compound sentence can be two sentences joined with a comma and a coordinate conjunction. Common coordinate conjunctions are **and, but, for, nor, or, yet,** and **so.**

Jaxson threw the ball to Cosmo, **but** Cosmo missed it.

Match a simple sentence in Column A with a simple sentence in Column B to create a compound sentence. Write the letter from Column B on the line.

Column A

1. ______ The first Wimbledon was played in 1877,
2. ______ There are four annual tennis tournaments known as "Grand Slams,"
3. ______ The game of tennis wasn't well known,
4. ______ Winners just won a trophy until 1968,
5. ______ Strawberries and cream are commonly enjoyed at Wimbledon,

Column B

a. for there wasn't any money to award as a prize.

b. and all white clothing is a tradition too.

c. and it is the oldest tennis tournament.

d. so the crowd for the first Wimbledon was small.

e. but Wimbledon is the only one to still be played on grass.

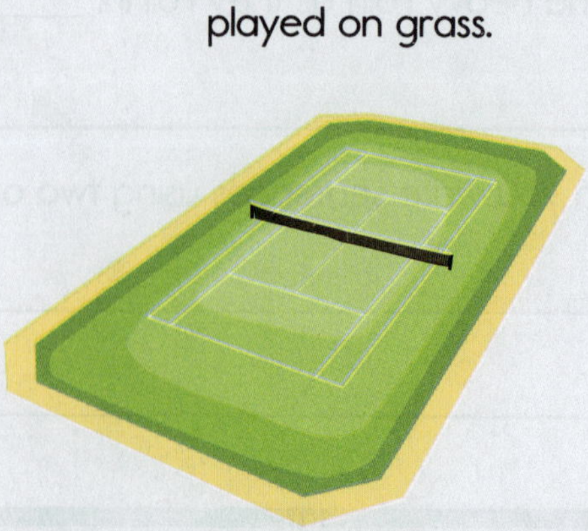

Name ____________________

Lesson 2.2 Simple and Compound Sentences

Read each sentence and determine whether it is a simple or compound sentence. On the line at the beginning of the sentence, write **S** for simple or **C** for compound. On the two lines following the sentence, identify the total number of subjects and predicates in each sentence.

1. ______ The starter blew the horn, and the dog ran down the ramp. **S:** ______ **P:** ______

2. ______ The East Pirates and the Westside Wildcats played each other last week, but tomorrow's game will be the regional championship. **S:** ______ **P:** ______

3. ______ Erin threw the ball high and aced her opponent. **S:** ______ **P:** ______

4. ______ Brandon played the violin, but his sister played the flute. **S:** ______ **P:** ______

5. ______ The concert was amazing, for Sasha's solo was beautiful. **S:** ______ **P:** ______

6. ______ The hostess seated our family and handed us menus. **S:** ______ **P:** ______

Can you write a paragraph about a hobby you like? Try it. Include a variety of simple and compound sentences.

____

____

____

____

____

Name ______________________________

Lesson 2.3 Complex Sentences

A **dependent clause** does not present a complete thought and cannot stand alone as a sentence.

Complex sentences have one independent clause and one or more dependent clauses. The independent and dependent clauses are connected with a subordinate conjunction or a relative pronoun.

Complex sentence (connected with subordinate conjunction):

I like reading historical fiction **because** it transports me to another place in time.

Complex sentence (connected with a relative pronoun):

Most people have heard of Steve Jobs, **who** was a co-founder of Apple.

The dependent clause can either be the first or second part of the sentence.

Before you play cornhole, you need to set up the boards.

You need to set up the boards **before you can play cornhole.**

For each unfinished complex sentence, choose a subordinate conjunction from the list and use it to create the rest of the sentence. Use a different word from the list for each sentence.

after	if	unless	where
although	once	until	wherever
because	since	when	whether
before	though	whenever	while

1. ______________________________, Jody will come over for a walk.

2. The rain poured down outside our window ______________________________.

3. My neighbor dug up all of her bushes ______________________________.

4. The rancher rounded up his cattle ______________________________.

5. I am supposed to walk home from school ______________________________.

6. ______________________________, the golf team departed from the school.

Name ______________________________

Lesson 2.3 Complex Sentences

For each sentence, circle the subordinate conjunction and underline the dependent clause.

1. Anish Kapoor's famous sculpture is called Cloud Gate, although most people refer to it as "The Bean."

2. When you are in Chicago, you should visit the beautiful, mirrored sculpture.

3. While some visitors stand close to it, others like to stand further away.

4. The sculptor lived in India until he moved to Britain in the early 1970s.

5. Once when I visited The Bean, it was so crowded I couldn't get very close.

6. Because of its arched shape, visitors can walk under the sculpture.

7. The reflection of the Chicago skyline in The Bean is distorted because of its shape.

8. Since The Bean is in Millennium Park, you'll be close to Lake Michigan, restaurants, shops, hotels, and more if you visit it.

Write four complex sentences on the lines below. Use subordinate conjunctions in two of them and relative pronouns in the other two.

9. ______________________________

10. ______________________________

11. ______________________________

12. ______________________________

Name ___________________________________

Lesson 2.4 Adjective and Adverb Clauses

An **adjective clause** is a dependent clause that modifies a noun or pronoun and usually follows the word it modifies. The clause begins with a relative pronoun, such as **that, which, who, whom, whose,** or **whoever.**

Our neighbor Jackson, **who works at the golf course,** just turned 16.
Terry drives a truck **that is too tall to fit into his garage.**

An **adverb clause** is a dependent clause that modifies a verb, an adjective, or an adverb. It answers the question **How? When? Where? Why?** or **Under what condition?** The first word of an adverb clause is a subordinate conjunction, such as **although, until, once, however, unless, if,** or **while.**

Until the test on Friday, I will study every night.
We're going morel mushroom hunting today **if it isn't raining.**

Choose a relative pronoun or subordinate conjunction from the word banks to complete each sentence.

Relative Pronouns				
whom	which	that	whoever	who

Subordinate Conjunctions				
when	unless	if	whenever	while

1. My moonflowers, ____________________ **are my favorite flowers,** are underneath our kitchen window.

2. Moonflowers only bloom ____________________ **the moon is out.**

3. ____________________ **the sun is out,** moonflowers close up.

4. ____________________ you **stand close to them,** you can smell their sweet fragrance.

5. Moonflowers are flowers ____________________ **you plant once and they bloom annually.**

6. My neighbor, ____________________ **is a master gardener,** has moonflowers in her backyard.

Name ___________________________

Lesson 2.4 Adjective and Adverb Clauses

Circle adjective clauses. Underline adverb clauses.

1. Have you heard of African wild dogs, which live near the Sahara Desert?

2. Somehow they survive in this African region that has very hot and dry conditions.
3. They often find grasslands that offer shelter from the sun.
4. Wild dogs, which hunt in packs of 15 to 60, prey on antelopes and other large animals.
5. While most wild dogs share a long, thin body, each one has unique markings in its fur.
6. Wild dogs have large ears that give it an acute sense of hearing.
7. Wild dogs are animals that are extremely vocal, using chirps and tweets to communicate with each other.
8. Although they bear a resemblance to domesticated dogs, they are wild and ferocious.

Would you want to see a wild dog in its habitat? Explain why or why not. Use adjective and/or adverb clauses in your answer.

____

____

____

____

Name ___________________________________

Review Chapter 2

On the line, identify the sentence type as **D** for declarative, IM for imperative, **IN** for interrogative, or **E** for exclamatory.

1. Have you ever been to the Shedd Aquarium in Chicago? ______
2. Built on the shore of Lake Michigan, this aquarium is amazing! ______
3. During a visit you can see beluga whales, penguins, alligators, sea turtles, and more. ______
4. Every year, more than two million people visit Shedd Aquarium! ______
5. The beautiful building, made of white marble, opened in 1930. ______
6. Shedd Aquarium offers the opportunity to touch and stand next to a beluga whale! ______
7. Can you picture yourself getting close to a beluga whale? ______
8. Go to the Shedd Aquarium the next time you are near Chicago. ______

Identify each sentence below as simple (**S**) or compound (**C**).

9. ______ Visitors at Shedd Aquarium can encounter sea lions up close and meet sea otters.
10. ______ The sea lion encounter is fun, but it also teaches about the challenges sea lions face in the wild.
11. ______ You can take a selfie with penguins, so you'll want to have a camera.
12. ______ Beautiful, tropical fish swim playfully around in the large aquarium, and tiny seahorses float gracefully along.

13. ______ Shedd Aquarium holds over 5 million gallons of water for its 30,000 different sea animals.
14. ______ Tour guides walk visitors around the aquarium and answer questions, and playful sea animals entertain guests with their enchanting behavior.

Name ____

Review Chapter 2

Underline the dependent clause in each complex sentence.

15. Although our flight was delayed, we still left for the airport.

16. Whenever my cousin goes swimming, she gets an earache.

17. The boat will take us to Ellis Island after we stop at the Statue of Liberty.

18. Unless you brought sunscreen with you, you might want to stay in the shade.

19. Roxie doesn't eat her breakfast when she has a stomachache.

20. Lana waited in the car while her dad went into the grocery store.

Circle the adjective clauses. Underline the adverb clauses.

21. Greyhounds, which are tall, thin dogs, are great family pets.

22. Although greyhounds are large dogs, they are known as gentle giants.

23. Even though greyhounds are known for their racing, they require little exercise as pets.

24. The greyhound, which is the fastest dog breed in the world, can run up to 45mph.

25. Greyhounds are dogs that are sensitive to temperature changes.

26. Because they are often surrendered when they can't race anymore, many loving greyhounds can be found at shelters and rescues.

27. Write a complex sentence.

____

28. Write a sentence with an adjective clause.

____

Chapter 3: Capitalization

Chapter 3 focuses on capitalization. Students will encounter capitalization with everything they write, from essays and reports to emails and letters. Knowing the rules of capitalization will help students form sentences and paragraphs that are easy for readers to follow and understand.

In this chapter, students will practice capitalization rules regarding dialogue, parts of a letter, and proper nouns. With dialogue, correct capitalization (in addition to the quotation marks) will help the reader determine where spoken words and sentences are beginning and ending. Especially when dialogue bounces back and forth between multiple speakers, it is important for it to be capitalized (and punctuated) correctly for clarity.

While casual emailing and texting have become more common than formal letter writing, knowing how to correctly capitalize parts of a letter is a skill that students will be glad they've learned when it is time to send out letters, applications, and resumes for scholarships, higher education, and/or jobs. This chapter gives students practice in correctly capitalizing the main parts of a personal and business letter, including the header, salutation, and closing.

Capitalizing proper nouns is addressed in Chapter 3 as well. Going beyond the general rule of capitalizing proper names, places, and things, Chapter 3 includes titles of books, poems, songs, movies, plays, newspapers, and magazines. It includes information on when to capitalize people's titles, such as Mayor Davis or Officer Ralston (but not "he was the mayor of Cincinnati"), names of governmental departments, organizations, historical events and documents, languages, sports teams, and more.

Skills Checklist

- ☐ Capitalizing the first word in a sentence
- ☐ Capitalizing words in quotations and dialogue
- ☐ Capitalizing parts of a letter (heading, salutation, closing)
- ☐ Capitalizing proper nouns (names, titles, organizations, periods in time, languages, sports teams, etc.)

Helpful Definitions

direct quotation: exact words that someone speaks; enclosed with quotation marks; Example: *"I would like a turkey sandwich," said Micah.*

indirect quotation: words that are not directly spoken; not enclosed with quotation marks; Example: *Micah said that he would like a turkey sandwich.*

heading: the part of a letter that includes the street name, city, state, and date; Example: *1717 View Drive, Grand Haven, MI 49417*

salutation: the part of a letter located right before the body text; names who is receiving the letter; Examples: *Dear Tracie, To whom it may concern*

closing: the part of a letter located right after the body text; a way to sign off or say goodbye; Examples: *Respectfully, Sincerely, Your friend,*

proper noun: names a specific person, place, or thing; always capitalized; Examples: *Texas, Mr. Stevens, Jupiter*

Name ______________________________

Lesson 3.1 Capitalization: Sentences and Quotations

Capitalize the first word of **every sentence.**

Honeybees are extremely important for the environment and agriculture.

Capitalize the first word in **direct quotations.**

"**Did** I leave my phone at your house?" asked Delilah.

Do not capitalize indirect quotations.

My English teacher said that I got the highest grade on the test.

If a continuous sentence in a direct quotation is split and the second half is not a new sentence, do not capitalize it.

"I want to go to the carnival," said Aaron, "**but** it's supposed to storm."

If a new sentence begins after the split, then capitalize it.

"My tooth hurts," said Reyna. "**It** hurts to chew on the right side of my mouth."

Rewrite each sentence using correct capitalization.

1. "did anyone feed Bubbles?" asked Mom.

____

2. "when you get home," said Leticia, "Please tell Mom that I'm staying for gymnastics practice."

____

3. "The tree blew over on our shed," said Dad. "i'll call tomorrow to have it removed."

____

4. "we're going to the gym in ten minutes!" yelled Padma. "does anyone want to come?"

____

Explain how correct punctuation in quotations makes the dialogue easier to understand.

____

____

Name ____

Lesson 3.1 Capitalization: Sentences and Quotations

Circle the letter of the sentence that is capitalized correctly.

1. **a.** the pool closed early due to the impending thunderstorm.

b. The pool closed early due to the impending thunderstorm.

2. **a.** "can I please have the receipt from the store?" asked Mom.

b. "Can I please have the receipt from the store?" Asked Mom.

c. "Can I please have the receipt from the store?" asked Mom.

3. **a.** "If you go hiking this afternoon," said Dad, "be sure to take water."

b. "If you go hiking this afternoon," said Dad, "Be sure to take water."

c. "if you go hiking this afternoon," said Dad, "be sure to take water."

4. **a.** As the storm approached, people boarded up their windows and secured their patio furniture.

b. as the storm approached, people boarded up their windows and secured their patio furniture.

5. **a.** "thank you for coming," said Dr. Betz, "as I am really excited to present to you today."

b. "Thank you for coming," said Dr. Betz, "As I am really excited to present to you today."

c. "Thank you for coming," said Dr. Betz, "as I am really excited to present to you today."

Can you write two quotations with correct capitalization? Try it.

1. ____

2. ____

Name ______________________________

Lesson 3.2 Capitalization: Letter Parts

When you write a letter, certain parts of it need to be capitalized.

Capitalize the **heading** of a letter. This includes the name of the street, the city, the state, and the month in the heading. This is at the top of the letter.

1645 Argentina Drive
Huntsville, Alabama 45213
April 5, 2023

Capitalize the first word of the **salutation**, or the name of the person who is receiving the letter. This is just before the body of the letter.

To whom it may concern: **Dear** Raj,

Also, capitalize the first word of the **closing**. This is after the body of the letter.

Your friend, **Sincerely,**

Fill in the missing parts of this personal letter using the word bank for your answers. Add capital letters where needed.

dear elijah,	your friend, trudy	1879 fruitvale road hot springs, arkansas 76212 june 2, 2023

____
____
____

____

Hi! I've been wanting to write to you since you moved away. Now that I don't have you living next door, I've been going to the park a lot to play with friends. I'm glad you're coming back to visit in a few months. Can't wait to see you! Give Snuggles a hug from me!

____
____

Name ______________________________

Lesson 3.2 Capitalization: Letter Parts

Proofread the following business letter for mistakes in capitalization. Underline a lowercase letter three times to make it a capital letter.

m capitalize a letter

office of parks and recreation
3215 148th avenue
dover, new hampshire 12745

october 25, 2023

to whom it may concern,

I live about 10 minutes from the Dover Community Trail. my family and I love to ride bikes and hike on the trails, have picnics near the trails, and walk our dog Angus on the trails. but lately we've noticed a large amount of trash along the trails and even floating down the river that runs along the trails. seeing all the trash is upsetting and it is hazardous to the animals that live in the woods. we've picked up some trash when we've seen some, but I'm wondering if your department has an organized clean-up day each month. the four of us can pick up a small amount of trash, but a large group can pick up a lot and make a bigger impact. if there is a designated day, we'd be happy to join in. If not, I hope your office will consider starting a monthly clean-up day. please let me know!

sincerely,

Alex Rodrigo

Explain how the letter above is difficult to read without correct capitalization.

____

____

Name ______________________________

Lesson 3.3 Capitalization: Names, Titles, and Places

Proper nouns are specific people, places, and things. Proper nouns are capitalized.

The class greeted **Brownie**, Kylie's new service dog. (specific person/pet)
The mountains in **Montana** are stunning. (specific place)
My favorite brand of yogurt is **Yoplait**. (specific thing)

The titles of books, poems, songs, movies, plays, newspapers, and magazines are proper nouns and are capitalized. In a title, capitalize all words except **a, an**, and **the** (unless it's the first word of the title). Do not capitalize short prepositions such as **of, to, in, on**, and **so**.

Most titles are also underlined or set in italic font in text. Song titles, essays, poems, and other shorter works are placed in quotes.

I am reading *To Kill a Mockingbird.*   We learned how to play "Sleigh Ride" in band.

Titles associated with names are capitalized, but do not capitalize these titles if they are not directly used with the name.

Mayor Richard M. Daley served as **mayor** of Chicago from 1989 to 2011.
David hopes to become a **professor** like **Professor** Nemechek.

Answer each question with a complete sentence. Use the correct punctuation.

1. What is the last movie you saw?

2. What city, state, or country would you like to visit?

3. What is your favorite song?

4. What brand of shoes or clothes do you like?

5. What is the last book you read?

Name ____

Lesson 3.3 Capitalization: Names, Titles, and Places

Correct the mistakes in capitalization using the proofreading mark. Underline a lowercase letter three times to make it a capital letter.

m (underlined three times) **capitalize a letter**

Have you ever been to our nation's capital? If not, washington, dc, should be on your list of places to visit. There is so much to see and do in this bustling, beautiful district that borders virginia and maryland. The Metro will take you all around the city, from the national museum of american history to the smithsonian national zoo. And best of all, many of the most popular sights, like the lincoln memorial and jefferson memorial, are free to visit!

Are you interested in space exploration? If so, the air and space museum is for you! Here, you can see the wright flyer, which was the first airplane built by orville and wilbur wright. You can also see charles lindbergh's spirit of st. louis, which was the first aircraft to fly nonstop from new york to paris. Also in this museum is neil armstrong's spacesuit that he wore on the apollo 17 mission. You could spend all day in this museum!

Would you like to see where george and martha washington lived? Just outside of washington, dc, is their historic estate called mount vernon. situated beautifully on the potomac river, the breathtaking grounds include the mansion, gardens, a riding stable, slave memorial, smoke house, ice house, and more. This 500-acre estate in virginia, as well as famous landmarks like the capitol in washington, dc, should be on everyone's list of places to visit in and around our nation's capital.

Name ____

Lesson 3.4 Capitalization: Other Proper Nouns

Organizations, departments of government, and sections of the country are all **proper nouns** and are capitalized.
The names of organizations, associations, and businesses are capitalized.

Carolina Waterfowl Rescue **The Rotary Club** **Nike**
Department of Education **Department of Homeland Security**

Directional words that point out particular sections of the country are capitalized. However, the words that give directions are not capitalized.

The **West** is experiencing many wildfires this summer.
My uncle lives **west** of the Rockies.

Historical events, periods of time, nationalities, important documents from history, and team names are proper nouns as well.
Jenna studied the **Civil War** in college. Max Scherzer used to pitch for the **Detroit Tigers.**

Names of languages and nationalities are capitalized. They are also capitalized when they are used as adjectives.

I have my **Latin** test on Monday.

Circle the words that should be capitalized.

1. I asked to have my sandwich made on french bread.

2. My friend is moving to the east coast when school gets out.

3. The lions club had a float in the parade.

4. The detroit lions are supposed to have a strong team this coming year.

5. The industrial revolution transformed North America and Europe to urban societies.

6. The department of agriculture oversees laws that pertain to farming and forestry.

Name ______________________________

Lesson 3.4 Capitalization: Other Proper Nouns

Complete each sentence below with a proper noun. Use the internet or ask someone for help if needed.

1. American forces defeated the British in the ____________________ (name of a war).

2. I would like to visit ____________________ (name of state) on the ____________________ (directional word) Coast.

3. The United States ____________________ (branch of the federal government) consists of nine judges.

4. The ____________________ (historical document) guarantees certain freedoms for United States citizens.

5. During the ____________________ (name of war), Abraham Lincoln gave his famous ____________________ (historical speech).

6. The United States entered ____________________ (name of a war) after Japan attacked Pearl Harbor.

7. I already know how to speak ____________________ (language), but I would love to learn ____________________ (language).

8. ____________________ (language) tea cakes are a popular holiday cookie.

9. ____________________ (company name) first introduced the iPod in 2001.

10. I am a member of ____________________ (name of club), but I would also like to join ____________________ (name of club).

Can you think of a way to describe yourself using a geographical word, like Cuban, Japanese, or German? Try it. Write a sentence about yourself.

____

Name ______________________________

Review Chapter 3

Proofread each sentence for capitalization. Use the proofreading marks.

m with three lines under it: **capitalize a letter**	M with a slash through it: **lowercase a letter**

1. Mika grew up on the west coast, but after College he moved to New Hampshire.

2. Vicki is italian, although she does not speak the Language fluently.

3. Mrs. chang's first article appeared in *photography today* magazine.

4. My Aunt bought my favorite cereal called green earth granola.

5. To reach the wilton museum of arts and crafts, turn West on broad street.

6. Did you know that six Presidents have been named James?

7. Donita plans to be a Doctor someday, but she hasn't decided on a specialty yet.

8. Did you know that portuguese is the official language of brazil?

9. Mom doesn't follow professional sports, but she's a big fan of the carolina tarheels.

10. Next summer, the kim family plans to visit grand canyon national park in arizona.

Name ____

Review Chapter 3

Read each letter part. If it is correct, make a check mark on the line. If it is incorrect, make an X on the line.

11. ______ Seattle, WA 98107

12. ______ Yours Truly,

13. ______ To Whom It May Concern:

14. ______ Mount vernon, OH 43050

15. ______ Dear Louis,

16. ______ Sincerely,

17. ______ November 14, 2023

18. ______ your friend,

Read each sentence. Write the word that should be capitalized on the line.

19. I will be taking spanish next year in eighth grade. ____________________

20. Mr. Gibbs served in the U.S. senate for twenty-two years. ____________________

21. Is mayor Rodriguez running again next year? ____________________

22. We were assigned the classic novel *emma* by Jane Austen. ____________________

Name ______________________________

Learning Checkpoint Chapters 1–3

There are ten errors in the paragraph. After you find them, write the words correctly on the lines.

Have you ever wanted to go to costa rica? Costa Rica is located in south America. It is known for its rainforests, volcanoes, and abundant wildlife species. The countrys most well-known animals are the sloth, toucan, monkeys, and red-eyed tree frog. Each has its own characteristics that makes them unique. The sloth, that hangs upside down for hours each day, exudes the laid-back lifestyle of the country. The toucan, with its huge, colorful beak, can easily be spotted in the lush, green rainforest. You'll hear the monkeys before you see it. Their screeching and howling echoes through the rainforest. For anyone who see a red-eyed tree frog, they will be amazed by its large red eyes and beautiful colors. The red-eyed tree frog uses its bright colors to camouflage themselves. These animals homes can be found in tortuguero national park and throughout the beautiful country of Costa Rica.

1. ______________________ **2.** ______________________

3. ______________________ **4.** ______________________

5. ______________________ **6.** ______________________

7. ______________________ **8.** ______________________

9. ______________________ **10.** ______________________

Name ______________________________

Learning Checkpoint Chapters 1–3

Complete each sentence with a verb that makes sense. Circle the sentence with the linking verb.

11. Every morning, I ____________________ yogurt and granola for breakfast.

12. When Hamilton comes to town, my mom and I ____________________ ____________________ to see it.

13. The cake that my mom just took out of the oven ____________________ delicious.

Underline the verb in each sentence. Then write on the line if it is a gerund (**G**), participle (**P**), or infinitive (**I**).

14. To mow the lawn on a clean air action day is bad for the environment. ______

15. The humming air conditioner was getting louder every day. ______

16. Talking is my Aunt Carolyn's favorite pastime. ______

17. Jacob's modified muffler on his car caused noise pollution. ______

Underline the verb(s) in each sentence. Circle the tense in parentheses for each verb.

18. I watch my dad bake my favorite cookies. (present, past, future)

19. He added extra chocolate chips. (present, past, future)

20. The cookies will be done in about 12 minutes. (present, past, future)

Name ______________________________

Learning Checkpoint Chapters 1–3

Underline the adjective in each sentence. On the line, write whether it is a proper, predicate, comparative, or superlative adjective.

21. The sandpaper felt scratchy against my skin. ______________________

22. They say a team is only as strong as its weakest link. ______________________

23. My friend, Gabriella, wears Italian shoes. ______________________

24. My dog is always softer after his bath. ______________________

Add an adverb or intensifier to each sentence.

25. The train was ________________ getting into the train station, so my mom was ________________ frustrated.

26. Tony's soccer cleats were ________________ smelly to keep in the house.

27. The audience ________________ gasped when the lights went out.

Complete each sentence by adding a preposition that makes sense. Underline the conjunction in the one sentence.

28. The captain went ________________ deck to see where the smoke was coming from.

29. I could see the commotion ________________ my bedroom window.

30. As long as there are squirrels in the yard, our dog will chase them ________________ the woods.

Name ____

Learning Checkpoint Chapters 1–3

Identify each sentence as a declarative (**D**), imperative (**IM**), interrogative (**IN**), or exclamatory (**E**) sentence.

31. "Wow, I think I just saw a UFO!" yelled Max. ______

32. "Are you joking?" asked Felipe. ______

33. "No, it was right up there," Max pointed into the night sky. ______

34. "Get your dad in case it comes back," said Felipe. ______

Circle whether the sentence is simple, compound, or complex.

35. Mia and Eryn both worked late into the evening. (simple, compound, complex)

36. Before your friends play pickleball, you need to teach them the rules. (simple, compound, complex)

37. Eryn was glad she was earning more money, but Mia just wanted to go home. (simple, compound, complex)

38. I handed my card to the librarian, who was standing behind the desk. (simple, compound, complex)

Underline the adjective or adverb clause in each sentence. Write on the line which type it is.

39. We live in a house that is too small for our family of five. ________________

40. When I have enough money saved up, I am going to buy new shoes. ________________

Name ______________________________

Learning Checkpoint Chapters 1–3

Circle the letter of the sentence that is capitalized correctly.

41. **a.** "I need to return my shirt," said Jones. "It doesn't fit."

b. "I need to return my shirt," said Jones. "it doesn't fit."

c. "I need to return my shirt," Said Jones. "It doesn't fit."

42. **a.** My swim coach said, "That I should start lifting weights to build muscle."

b. My swim coach said "That I should start lifting weights to build muscle."

c. My swim coach said that I should start lifting weights to build muscle.

43. **a.** "Levon, do you have an extra picture order form?" Asked Carlyn.

b. "Levon, Do you have an extra picture order form?" asked Carlyn.

c. "Levon, do you have an extra picture order form?" asked Carlyn.

Rewrite these parts of a letter so they are capitalized correctly.

44. community mental health ______________________

12263 collin avenue ______________________

plainfield, illinois 60544 ______________________

45. august 1, 2023 ______________________

46. to whom it may concern, ______________________

47. regards, ______________________

Name ______________________________

Learning Checkpoint Chapters 1–3

If the underlined words are correct as punctuated (capital letters), put a check mark on the line. If they are incorrect, put an **X** on the line.

48. ______ The Governor of our state visited our school last week.

49. ______ My neighbor is a professor at the local community college.

50. ______ Trevor's aunt and uncle moved to Germany.

51. ______ Night At The Museum was filmed mostly in Canada.

52. ______ The Constitution, which was signed on September 17, 1787, established the government of the United States.

53. ______ The department of homeland security was founded in 2002 by president George W. Bush.

54. ______ The high school french teachers take a group of kids to France every other summer.

55. ______ It is believed that the Renaissance time period began in Italy during the 14th century.

56. ______ Washington's football team is now known as the Washington commanders.

57. ______ The beautiful Southwest is known for its deserts, red rock landscapes, and mountainous terrain.

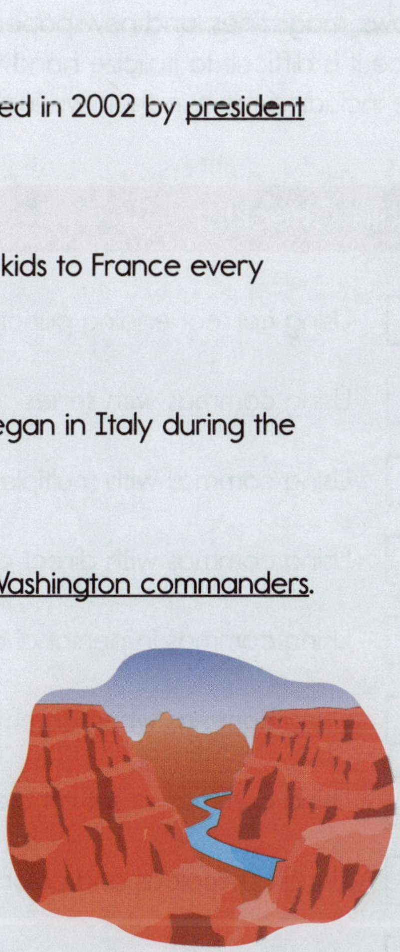

Chapter 4: Punctuation

Chapter 4 takes a look at the mechanics of writing, which includes ending punctuation marks, the various uses of commas, colons and semicolons, quotation marks, apostrophes, hyphens, dashes, parentheses, and the italicizing and underlining of titles.

After a quick review of ending punctuation marks, the chapter turns to the many ways commas are used in writing. This includes using commas with a series of items (eggs, bacon, and toast) and multiple adjectives (sweet, ripe strawberries), in direct address, in personal and business letters, when combining sentences, and to set off dialogue. The comma is small but mighty, its correct placement and inclusion very important to the flow and clarity of a sentence.

Students will also gain practice with the sometimes-confusing colon and semicolon. While not used as often as other marks, it's important for students to understand the reasons for using each one. Quotation marks and apostrophes are common in writing, and Chapter 4 gives students practice at punctuating dialogue, possessives, and contractions. Students will also be introduced to the correct usage of hyphens, dashes, and parentheses. When used in writing, they can add variety and interest to sentences and paragraphs. Finally, the rule of italicizing and/or underlining of titles is covered. This includes titles of books, plays, movies, TV shows, magazines, and newspapers. Students will almost always see these titles italicized. But since it is difficult to italicize handwriting, we suggest that students underline them when they are including them in their writing. If typing, then they can italicize them.

Skills Checklist

- [ ] Using correct ending punctuation marks
- [ ] Using commas with series
- [ ] Using commas with multiple adjectives
- [ ] Using commas with direct address
- [ ] Using commas in personal and business letters
- [ ] Using commas when combining sentences
- [ ] Using commas to set off dialogue
- [ ] Using semicolons and colons
- [ ] Using quotation marks

☐ Using an apostrophe

☐ Using hyphens, dashes, and parentheses

☐ Using italics for titles of works

Helpful Definitions

series commas: used with three or more items listed in a sentence; Example: *There are birds, squirrels, and chipmunks in our yard.*

multiple adjectives: describe a noun and are separated by commas; Example: *The wet, slimy fish slipped through my hands.*

direct address: when someone is directly spoken to, commas are used to separate the name of the person from the rest of the sentence; Example: *"Mary, can you help me study for my test?"*

dialogue: conversation between people; set off with quotation marks; Example: *"Hi Jonah," said Hannah. "Hi Hannah," he replied.*

semicolon: used to join two independent clauses, or to separate clauses, series of words, or phrases when they contain commas; Example: *The waffles were so good; they were sweet and buttery.*

colon: used to introduce a series, set off a clause, set off a word or phrase for emphasis, in writing time, or after a salutation in a letter; Example: *The following students passed the test: Henry, Rosa, and Isobel.*

quotation marks: used to show the exact words of a speaker; placed before and after the exact words; Example: *"I'm ready for school," said Marcus.*

apostrophe: used in contractions, to form possessives, and to form plurals; Examples: *we've, Sasha's, parents'*

hyphen: used to divide words that come at the end of a line, used to divide compound numbers, used to divide some compound nouns; Examples: *forty-two, cutting-edge technology*

dash: used to separate a group of words; can indicate a sudden change in thought; Example: *Swimming in Brady's pool-which is huge-is so much fun!*

parentheses: used to call attention to additional material or to set off phrases in a strong way; Example: *My grandma (my mom's mom) is living with us.*

italics: a way to punctuate titles of books, plays, movies, TV shows, magazines, and newspapers; Examples: *Wonder, Hamilton, Frozen*

Name ______________________________

Lesson 4.1 Ending Punctuation Marks

Periods are used at the end of declarative sentences and some imperative sentences.

Sprinkling coyote urine around hostas will keep deer away.

Email your teacher about your test grade.

Question marks are used at the end of interrogative sentences.

Where are your golf clubs?

Who asked for the sandwich with mayonnaise?

Exclamation points are used at the end of exclamatory sentences. They are also used at the end of imperative sentences that show urgency, strong surprise, or emotion.

I got the lead role in the upcoming play!

Look at that owl!

Add an ending punctuation mark to each sentence below.

1. There are too many groceries in this bag ______
2. Oh no, the bag is ripping ______
3. Yikes, everything just broke on the ground ______
4. I'll go back inside and get a few new bags ______
5. Clean up what's spilled on the ground ______
6. Did the eggs break ______
7. Can you ask the cashier for a broom ______
8. Grab the can of corn, it's rolling away ______

Name ______________________________

Lesson 4.1 Ending Punctuation Marks

Circle the end mark that correctly completes each sentence.

1. Trade schools offer many courses of study (. ? !)
2. Have you ever been interested in learning a trade (. ? !)
3. If you want to become a chef, you can study culinary arts at a trade school (. ? !)
4. You could become a celebrity chef (. ? !)
5. Does graphic design sound interesting to you (. ? !)
6. Graphic design classes include digital and print media (. ? !)

7. Graphic designers often work remotely and can work in many industries (. ? !)
8. Do you like heavy machines (. ? !)
9. Driving a bulldozer for work would be awesome (. ? !)
10. If you like heavy equipment, maybe construction would be a good trade for you (. ? !)
11. With dozens of career options, trade schools are a great option (. ? !)

At a quick glance, what can ending punctuation tell us about a sentence?

____

____

Name ____

Lesson 4.2 Commas: Series, Multiple Adjectives

Series commas are used with three or more items listed in a sentence. The items can be words or phrases. They are separated by commas.

The countries with the largest populations are **India, China, and the United States.**

To make snickerdoodles, we'll need **butter, cinnamon, sugar, flour, and salt.**

When **multiple adjectives** describe a noun, they are separated by commas.

We picked **sweet, ripe** blueberries at the farm down the street.

Hannah painted her room in a **calm, soothing** blue.

Make sure the adjectives equally modify the noun (coordinate adjectives). If they do, you can switch the order without changing the meaning.

The **fast, expensive** car impressed everyone. (coordinate adjectives)

Zoe wore **shiny rubber** boots into the garden. (non-coordinate adjectives)

Read the sentences below. Add commas where they are needed. If the sentence is correct as is, make a check mark on the line.

1. ______ There was thunder lightning and hail during the rainstorm.

2. ______ The big burly man chopped the tree down with ease.

3. ______ We enjoyed the beautiful Brazilian beach on vacation.

4. ______ Jeanine grabbed eggs bacon hashbrowns and a donut from the buffet.

5. ______ Jonah's smelly old soccer cleats stunk up the house.

6. ______ Adrian found a coin, a ring and some keys with his metal detector.

Name ____

Lesson 4.2 Commas: Series, Multiple Adjectives

Decide what kind of comma (if any) is needed in each sentence. Write the letter of your answer on the line. Then add the commas.

a. series comma **b.** multiple adjectives comma **c.** no comma needed

1. ______ Our local library offers programs about gardening crafting and scrapbooking.
2. ______ Meetings for the programs are often held in a large open conference room.
3. ______ There are many interested people who attend each week.
4. ______ For the gardening program, we learned about weeding planting and fertilizing.
5. ______ The crafting program included a fun sock puppet project.
6. ______ Very creative enthusiastic people come for the scrapbooking projects.
7. ______ The library is open late on Monday Tuesday and Thursday evenings.

8. ______ Next year the library is offering classes about photography sketching and painting.

Can you write your own sentences with commas? Try it! Write the type that is indicated in the parentheses.

1. (series comma)

____

2. (multiple adjectives)

____

Name ______________________________

Lesson 4.3 Commas: In Direct Address

In **direct address**, commas are used to separate the name of a person spoken to from the rest of the sentence.
When a name occurs at the beginning or ending of a sentence, one comma is used.

Anton, when is your band concert?

Your order is ready**, Mrs. Ruiz.**

When a name occurs in the middle of a sentence, two commas are used.

I highly doubt, **Michael,** that you've cleaned your room today.

Use the proofreading mark to add commas where needed in these sentences with direct address.

^, **inserts comma**

1. Moxie come back here!
2. If you know the answer DiMarco raise your hand.
3. I ordered you a thin-crust veggie pizza Ally.
4. Carlos do you want to go to the park after school?
5. Have I ever led you astray before Dom?
6. Mr. Llewellyn have you graded my paper yet?
7. If you have a moment Emry I'd like to speak with you.
8. Congratulations Jon you earned first chair in the saxophone section.

Can you write sentences with direct address? Try it. Make sure you add the comma(s) where needed.

1. ______________________________

2. ______________________________

Name ______________________________

Lesson 4.4 Commas: Personal and Business Letters

Commas are used in both **personal** and **business letters.**

Personal Letters

Commas appear in four of the five parts of a personal letter.

Heading:	**2393 River Road** **Cheboygan, MI 49721** **July 2, 2023**
Salutation:	**Dear Pilar,**
Body:	**comma usage** **in sentences**
Closing:	**Your friend,**

Business Letters

Commas appear in four of the six parts of a business letter.

Heading:	**1006 Dilly Drive** **Roanoke, VA 24005** **October 25, 2023**
Inside Address:	**Mrs. Cathryn Humphrey** **2398 Newport Road** **Roanoke, VA 24005**
Body:	**comma usage** **in sentences**
Closing:	**Regards,**

Rewrite each item below. Include commas where they are needed.

1. Your friend ______________________________

2. June 7 2023 ______________________________

3. I have a degree in Biology and I am very interested in applying for this job.

   ____

4. Sincerely ______________________________

5. San Francisco CA 94109 ______________________________

6. When we visited my grandma we took cookies to her.

   ____

7. Dear Aunt Rachael ______________________________

8. All my love ______________________________

9. December 23 2023 ______________________________

10. Charlotte NC 28201 ______________________________

Name ______________________________

Lesson 4.5 Commas: Combining Sentences

Use a comma to **combine two independent clauses** with a coordinate conjunction.

My mom handed me a thoughtful note**, and** I cried after reading it.

In a complex sentence, **connect a dependent and an independent clause** with a comma and subordinate conjunction.

Because I hadn't eaten breakfast, I didn't have the energy to run the 5K.

If the sentence is correct, write **C** on the line. If it is incorrect, write **X** on the line and use the proofreading mark to add a comma.

^, **inserts comma**

1. ______ Kenya is in East Africa which is on the Indian Ocean.

2. ______ Although part of its landscape is a savanna it also has mountains and plateaus.

3. ______ There are more than 60 languages spoken in Kenya and almost everyone speaks more than one.

4. ______ Because Kenya is home to so many beautiful animal species the government has established more than 50 reserves to protect them.

5. ______ Because bones of one of the earliest human ancestors were found in Kenya, scientists wonder if humans originated here.

6. ______ During the 1600s and 1700s, many Kenyans were taken as enslaved people by Americans, Europeans, and Arabs.

Can you write two sentences that use commas to combine sentences? Try it.

1. (two independent clauses) ______________________________

____

2. (one dependent and one independent clause) ______________________________

____

Name ________________________________

Lesson 4.5 Commas: Combining Sentences

This story is missing commas that combine sentences together. Add the missing commas using the proofreading mark.

^ inserts comma

Have you visited Niagara Falls? If you haven't you should see this natural wonder. Niagara Falls isn't just one waterfall it is three humongous waterfalls. There are two waterfalls on the American side and one waterfall on the Canadian side. Because each one is beautiful in its own way you should really see all three.

Niagara Falls was formed by glaciers melting during the last Ice Age which was around 12,000 years ago. Over 700,000 gallons of water per second flow over the falls which makes it the largest waterfall in North America in volume. If you measured its speed the water rushes at 25 miles per hour!

All of this powerful, rushing water is put to good use thanks to Nikola Tesla and George Westinghouse. They created the world's first hydroelectric power plant that uses the water to generate electricity! The water from Niagara Falls generates 4 million kilowatts of electricity which powers a quarter of the state of New York and Ontario, Canada.

People have plunged over the falls on purpose but most have not survived. Fish often flow over the falls with the water and they have a higher survival rate than humans.

If you plan to visit these stunning falls bring a camera and a raincoat. The spray from the falls often gives visitors a cool shower.

Did you learn something new about Niagara Falls? Write it below, using two sentences combined together.

____

____

Name ______________________________

Lesson 4.6 Commas: To Set Off Dialogue

Commas are used when **setting off dialogue** from the rest of the sentence.

Aunt Sasha yelled, "You forgot your wallet!"

"When you find the answer," said Dad, "call to me and I'll come check it."

Add commas where needed in the dialogue.

^, **inserts comma**

1. "Grab your pencils " said our teacher "we are going to take a short quiz."

2. "I haven't read any of the chapters that were assigned " Jalen said nervously.

3. "This unit is so hard " said Malek.

4. "If I pass this quiz " said Rosy "it'll be a miracle"

5. Trent smirked "Maybe you all should have paid more attention in class"

6. "I have paid attention " said Anton "but chemistry is so confusing."

7. "And Mrs. Bultman talks so fast, it's hard to keep up with my notes " said Bella.

8. "You have thirty minutes for the quiz " said Mrs. Bultman "and you can get started now."

Can you think of something you've recently said to someone? Write it below using quotation marks and a comma.

____

____

Name ______________________________

Lesson 4.6 Commas: To Set Off Dialogue

Add commas where they are needed using the proofreader mark. Fifteen commas are missing.

^ **inserts comma**

DeShaun walked out to the pool where his dad was reading a book.

"Hey Dad what are you doing?" he asked.

Looking up from his book, he replied "Reading a book."

Laughing, DeShaun said "I can see that, but I meant, what are you reading?"

"I'm reading a book about World War II " said his dad. "A young Italian boy is forced to spy on Hitler and his men. He learns about what they have planned and then brings back this information to the Italian government. He speaks Italian and German, so he's a perfect spy."

"Wow " said DeShaun "that sounds really good. Is it a true story?"

"It is " said his dad "which makes it even more interesting. I'm about halfway through it and I can't wait to see what happens."

"Can I borrow it when you're done " asked DeShaun "because I am looking for a new book to read?"

"Yes! If I get some alone time by the pool, I'll finish it faster " he said with a smirk.

"Oh, I get it " laughed DeShaun. "I'll go find someone else to talk to."

Explain why it is important for sentences to have the correct punctuation.

____

____

Name ____

Review Lessons 4.1–4.6

Add the correct ending punctuation mark to each sentence.

1. Do you know when school starts this fall ______
2. Wow, Mandy sent this text to 23 people ______
3. Get the mail, and leave it in the basket in the mud room ______
4. My friend asked me to dog sit for her this weekend ______
5. Do you hear that loud beeping noise ______

Add the missing commas to the letter.

1764 Echo St.
Des Moines IA 50301
July 31 2023

Mrs. Laura Santiago
7609 Coaster Rd.
Iowa City IA 52240

Dear Mrs. Santiago:

I am writing to you today to thank you your lifeguards and your emergency response team for helping my family on our most recent trip to your amusement park. It was a hot sunny day and temperatures were well into the 90s. While waiting in line for the Screamin' Sally waterslide, my dad felt lightheaded. He fell to the hot concrete ground hit his head and got a big nasty bump on his forehead. Many concerned people gathered around. Your response team raced over gently placed him on a big long stretcher and started administering first aid. Once they gave him water helped him cool down and got him back on his feet, he felt much better. Your team helped turn a scary unexpected event into an experience that turned out okay. Thank you!

Sincerely
Tatum White

Name ______________________________

Review Lessons 4.1–4.6

If the sentence is correct, put a check mark on the line. If it is missing a comma, add it where it is needed.

6. ______ Kevin do you want to meet in the park later today?

7. ______ "We fly out at 6am" said Alana "so we have to get up really early."

8. ______ My dog is scared of the water so we don't take him to the beach.

9. ______ If you feel ill, Trevor, you can call your grandma to come pick you up.

10. ______ Please take the trash out when you leave Reagan.

11. ______ Because of the extreme drought we can't water our grass every day.

12. ______ I heard the hooting, and I looked up and saw the owl looking down at me.

Write the sentences with correct punctuation and commas.

13. "Look out" yelled Marty. "Caleb has a 90 mph pitch"

____

14. Since I didn't do well on my first test. I will retake the test next week.

____

15. I was really tired last night. Yet I couldn't fall asleep for hours.

____

16. "What time is your cross country practice today" asked my dad

____

Name ____________________

Lesson 4.7 Semicolons and Colons

Colons have several functions in a sentence.
Colons are used to introduce a series in a sentence. Colons are not needed when the series is preceded by a verb or a preposition.

The Shakespeare Actor's Group performed in the following cities: **Roanoke, Christiansburg, and Blacksburg.**

My favorite popcorn flavors **are caramel apple, Wisconsin cheddar, and pizza.**

Colons are sometimes used instead of a comma to set off a clause.

We can't head out to sea: **the fog is too thick.**

Colons are used to set off a word or phrase for emphasis.

Pete heard growling and turned to see his worst nightmare: **a grizzly bear.**

Colons are used when writing the time.

The final exam begins at **9:00.**

Business letters use colons in the salutation—**Dear Sir or Madam:**

A semicolon is a cross between a period and a comma.
Semicolons join two independent clauses when a coordinate conjunction is not used.

I ate my dessert first; life is too short to eat dessert last.

Semicolons are used to separate clauses when they already contain commas.

For the beach we brought sandwiches, chips, and fruit; **water, soda, and tea; and a frisbee, beachball, and a volleyball.**

Rewrite the following sentences, adding colons or semicolons where needed.

1. Winds gusted over 50mph over night by morning, trees and power lines were down.

____

2. My mom gave me a list that had the following items on it laundry detergent, dog treats, orange juice, and ice cream.

____

3. This morning I downloaded a new payment app on my phone and deleted a notebook app I washed my car and I read two chapters in my new book.

____

4. You won't believe who I saw at the coffee shop Ed Sheeran.

____

Name ______________________________

Lesson 4.7 Semicolons and Colons

Colons and semicolons are missing or used incorrectly in these sentences. Rewrite each sentence correctly on the line.

1. A few animals that live in the savannas are: lions, elephants, wildebeests, and giraffes.

____

2. Savannas are tropical grasslands the grasses go dormant to survive in the extreme heat.

____

3. Savannas are hot all year long they have a wet and dry season.

____

4. Animals like zebras, lions, and antelopes move across the landscape looking for food: this is called migration.

____

5. Fires in the savanna benefit the landscape in many ways; they stop overcrowding of trees, help new grasses grow, and help some new plants grow.

____

6. Overgrazing and climate change is causing desertification this is bad for the animals and people who rely on the savanna.

____

7. Animals in the savanna have special survival traits elephants and giraffes have long trunks and necks to reach food.

____

8. Someday I want to visit the world's largest savanna the Serengeti in Africa.

____

Name ______________________________

Lesson 4.8 Quotation Marks

Quotation marks are used to show the exact words of a speaker. The quotation marks are placed before and after the exact words.

"**Did you pick up the cake?**" asked Leon. "**The party starts in an hour.**"

Quotation marks are also used when a direct quotation contains another direct quotation.

Henri explained, "*Mom said,* '**Give your permission slip to the office.**'"

Note the single quotation marks are used to set off the inside quotation. Single quotes express what Mom said. Double quotes express what Henri said.

Quotation marks are used with titles of short stories, poems, songs, and articles in magazines and newspapers.

Amanda Gorman read her poem "**The Hill We Climb**" at the 2021 presidential inauguration.

If a title is quoted within a direct quotation, then single quotation marks are used.

Melinda asked, "Have you read '**Flight**' by John Steinbeck?"

Add double or single quotation marks where they are needed in each sentence.

1. Can you tell me again, asked Mr. Brooks, which schools will be marching in the parade?
2. Marcus reminded me, Mrs. Greenwood said, You'll all have two tries on the experiment. If the first one fails, you can redo it.
3. My cousins and I love singing Grandma Got Run Over by a Reindeer around the holidays.
4. Janie, the receptionist said, Arrive 15 minutes before your appointment to fill out new-patient paperwork, said my mom.
5. The poem Be Glad Your Nose Is on Your Face by Jack Prelutsky makes me laugh, said Wilbur.

Can you write a sentence that uses double and single quotation marks? Try it.

____

____

Name ___________________________________

Lesson 4.8 Quotation Marks

The passage below contains several errors with quotation marks. Add quotation marks where they are needed using the proofreading mark.

" " inserts quotation marks

My English teacher Mr. Taylor said, Let's talk about poems today. Who has a favorite poem that they'd like to tell us the title of?

Miriam raised her hand and replied, My favorite poem is from Shel Silverstein's book Where the Sidewalk Ends. It's called the Homework Machine.

Thank you, Miriam. That's a funny one, said Mr. Taylor. Jesse, you have your hand up. What poem is your favorite? he asked.

My favorite poem is Jabberwocky by Lewis Carroll. It's full of nonsense words that are almost impossible to memorize, he said.

Oh yes, said Mr. Taylor. I had to recite part of Jabberwocky for an acting class I took when I was young. That is a difficult one.

My mom told me, If you can memorize and recite the entire poem to me, I'll take you out to lunch, said Jesse. I did it and she took me to our favorite Mexican restaurant.

Wow, that's great, said Mr. Taylor. Would you like to recite it to the class? he asked.

That was last year, said Jesse. I don't even think I'd remember the first line, he said, laughing.

Write a short dialogue between two friends discussing their favorite songs. Be sure to use single and double quotes where they are needed.

____

____

____

____

Name ______________________________

Lesson 4.9 Apostrophes

Apostrophes are used in contractions, to form possessives, and to form plurals. Apostrophes take the place of the omitted letters in contractions.

I will = I'll **could not = couldn't**

Possessives show possession, or ownership. To form the possessive of a singular noun, add an apostrophe and an **s**. This rule applies even if the noun already ends in **s**.

The **tree's** leaves were changing color. Is that **Louis's** notebook?

To form the possessive of plural nouns ending in **s**, add an apostrophe. If the plural noun does not end in **s**, add both the apostrophe and an **s**.

The **reviewers'** opinions about the video game can be read online.

The **women's** coats are located in the far corner of the store.

Read each sentence below. If the apostrophes are used correctly, make a check mark on the line. If they are used incorrectly or are missing, make an X on the line.

1. ______ Kammy's tai chi class was canceled for this afternoon.
2. ______ The parents applause grew louder as the graduates filed into the auditorium.
3. ______ I have'nt had time to do my homework all week.
4. ______ Cathryn's book club is meeting at the coffee shop this weekend.
5. ______ The banquet for the swim team will be at the Millers' house.
6. ______ The teacher ignored the students' groans and handed out the test anyway.

Name ______________________________

Lesson 4.9 Apostrophes

Each sentence below is missing at least one apostrophe. Add the apostrophes where they are needed using the proofreading mark.

✓ inserts apostrophe

1. Farmers across the country use cows manure as fertilizer.
2. What you probably havent heard, though, is that manure can be used to create power.
3. With a single cow producing about 30 gallons of manure a day, thats a lot of manure!
4. Scientists idea of using manure to create power is brilliant.
5. The manures dropped in a giant tank called a digester.
6. The digesters job is to collect gas that is given off by the manure, which can be turned into energy.
7. If a farmers crops dont do well one year, they can sell their manure energy.
8. Cow manure energy isn't a fossil fuel, so its not harmful to the environment.

Can you write one sentence that includes a contraction and one that includes a possessive? Try it.

____

____

Name ____

Lesson 4.10 Hyphens

Hyphens are used to divide words that come at the end of a line. Divide words between syllables.

The interior designer decorated our living room with a beautiful sofa and **pic-
tures** on the wall.

Do not divide one letter from the rest of the word, and divide syllables after the vowel if the vowel is a syllable by itself. Divide words with double consonants between the consonants.

admira-tion, not **a-dmiration** or **admir-ation** **fil-ling** **rid-dle**

Hyphens are used between compound numbers from twenty-one through ninety-nine.

Twenty-one people attended the professor's lecture.

Hyphens are used in compound modifiers only when the modifier precedes the word it modifies. Hyphens are not used for compound modifiers that include adverbs ending in **-ly.**

Our large Labrador is a **well-fed** dog. My dog is well fed.

I looked in the nest and saw four **fully hatched** baby birds.

Use hyphens in some compound nouns. You will need to check in a dictionary to be sure which compound nouns need hyphens.

Leslie was the **runner-up** in the spelling bee championship.

Add hyphens where they are needed in the following sentences. Use a dictionary if needed.

1. My sister in law, Mildred, is a self described neat freak.

2. I have twenty two dollars that I am keeping in
side my wallet until I find what I want to buy.

3. Luis told me a far fetched story that I didn't believe.

4. The Great Febrezio did a mind blowing stunt, and we were pleasantly sur
prised that he was ok.

5. I made sure my passport is up to date since we're traveling out of the country next month.

Name ______________________________

Lesson 4.10 Hyphens

Words in these sentences are missing hyphens. Rewrite the sentences with hyphens.

1. My great grandmother gave me her much loved cookbook.

____

2. My well worn cookie sheet looks like it's been used about ninety five times.

____

3. All summer long, most of the Southwest and West have had above average temperatures.

____

4. Our well stocked medicine cabinet includes bandages, over the counter medicine, antibiotic ointment, and cotton balls.

____

5. My brother told a knee slapping joke that had everyone laughing.

____

6. Mr. Yang is a clean cut man who dresses in business suits.

____

7. I have thirty one days left to use my twenty five dollar gift card.

____

8. My not so patient little cousin couldn't wait to go on the merry go round.

____

Write two sentences with words that have a hyphen.

9. ______________________________

10. ______________________________

Name ______________________________

Lesson 4.11 Dashes

A **dash** separates a group of words, not parts of a word like a hyphen, and it indicates a sudden break or change in thought. A dash can be used in place of a semicolon, parentheses, or words. A dash is longer than a hyphen.

We took our rabbit (her name is Lily) outside to run around in the backyard.
We took our rabbit–**her name is Lily**–outside to run around in the backyard.

I know who is knocking on my door; it's my neighbor.
I know who is knocking on my door–**it's my neighbor**.

Mary needed to pick up many things at the store, and they were eggs, milk, bread, and ice cream.
Mary needed to pick up many things at the store–**eggs, milk, bread, and ice cream.**

Match the sentence parts together by drawing lines between the words in Column B and the incomplete sentences in Column A.

Column A	Column B
1. The dense fog ________ makes it hard to see the nearby lighthouse.	–I need to apologize to my friend.
2. I know what I need to do ________.	–and I've thought about this for a while–
3. My decision ________ is that I don't feel it is safe for you to go.	–he needs to go to the vet.
4. Taylor Swift ________ writes all her songs herself.	–which is common along the coast of Maine–
5. My dog is sick ________.	–who started out in country music–

Name ______________________________

Lesson 4.11 Dashes

Rewrite each sentence by replacing a semicolon, parentheses, or words with a dash.

1. If I had to do it over again (which I can't) I would choose a different city to live in.

____

2. Elvis Presley (known as the "King of Rock and Roll") was only 42 years old when he died.

____

3. I'll text him today (even though he's on vacation) about the meeting next week.

____

4. I know what I want for my birthday; I want a trick scooter.

____

5. Mario knows what to order me and it's a chocolate mint milkshake.

____

6. Someday I hope to play at the oldest golf course in the world, and it is St. Andrews.

____

Name ______________________________

Lesson 4.12 Parentheses

Parentheses call attention to additional material or set off phrases in a stronger way than commas. By adding this information, it can add to the reader's understanding of the sentence. The additional information can be dates, numbers, acronyms, or more details or description about the topic.

On the first Tuesday of next month **(August 2)** there will be an open casting call.
The cost of the shoes **($125)** was well beyond what he could spend.
Tony Bennett **(winner of 20 Grammy Awards)** died in 2023.
The headquarters for the National Aeronautics and Space Administration **(NASA)** is in Washington, DC.

Rewrite each sentence by adding parentheses where they belong.

1. At 119° F 48° C, today was the hottest day on record in Phoenix, Arizona.

____

2. There are 107 Historically Black Colleges and Universities HBCUs in the United States.

____

3. The day of the attack on the United States Capitol January 6, 2021 was a low point in American history.

____

4. The text that Liberty sent me that I deleted wasn't very nice.

____

5. I wanted to go to Nashville because they have the best BBQ but nobody else wanted to go.

____

Name ______________________________

Lesson 4.12 Parentheses

Write your own sentences that contain parentheses.

1. (to add a date) ______________________________

____

2. (to add extra information about a person) ______________________________

____

3. (to add an acronym) ______________________________

____

4. (to add extra information about a thing) ______________________________

____

5. (to add a time) ______________________________

____

6. (to add extra information about a place) ______________________________

____

Do you think parentheses are used in formal or informal writing? Explain your answer.

____

____

Name ______________________________

Lesson 4.13 Using Italics and Underlining

When you are working on a computer, use **italics** for the titles of books, plays, movies, television series, magazines, and newspapers. If you are writing by hand, **underline** them.

Hatchet is a great book to read in middle school. (book)

Since we live near Chicago, my mom reads *The Chicago Sun Times* online. (newspaper)

My parents watch *Kitchen Wars* every week. (TV show)

Underline the title that should be italicized in each sentence.

1. Frank loves animals and nature, so he reads National Geographic Kids magazine.

2. Prisoner B-3087 is a historical fiction book about Holocaust prisoners.

3. My mom wants to be a contestant on Wheel of Fortune.

4. Hamilton is coming to town this fall and my grandpa is taking me to see it.

5. For my research paper on Rosa Parks, I put Who Is Rosa Parks? on hold at the library.

6. Tom Cruise does his own stunts in his Mission Impossible movies.

7. Have you ever watched a season of Survivor?

8. My uncle reads the USA Today online to learn about the day's biggest stories.

Explain why you think titles of works might be italicized (or underlined).

____

____

Name ________________________________

Lesson 4.13 Using Italics and Underlining

Answer each of the following questions with a complete sentence.

1. What book would you recommend to a friend?

____

2. What movie have you seen that is based on a book?

____

3. What magazine have you used for a school project or research paper?

____

4. If you could see a play, what would it be?

____

5. What is the title of a book near you right now?

____

6. What is the name of your hometown newspaper?

____

7. If you could get a subscription to a magazine, which magazine would it be?

____

8. What TV show do you look forward to watching?

____

Name ____________________

Review Lessons 4.7-4.13

Each sentence is missing a colon or semicolon. Write the correct punctuation mark on the line.

1. Please bring one of the following to the potluck ___ an appetizer, a salad, a drink, or a dessert.

2. You won't believe the new cookie flavor at the bakery ___ double chocolate peanut butter!

3. Kyle lost his work gloves ___ he doesn't remember where he left them.

4. The rain fell hard all night ___ in the morning, the street was flooded.

Add quotation marks, apostrophes, and other missing punctuation where it is needed in each sentence.

5. If I had ridden my bike faster, I wouldnt have gotten rained on said Azul.

6. Kaitlyn, my mom cant give you a ride home today, said Lyle.

7. The doctor said, You wont be able to run track until your ankle heals, said Anna.

8. I think I want to join the boys swim team this winter, said Rico.

9. Lucys skis and poles went flying everywhere yelled her friend, Dana.

10. The boys quick throw to first base finally ended the game.

Name ____

Review Lessons 4.7–4.13

Add a hyphen, dash, or parentheses where they are needed in each sentence.

11. Mr. Reynolds won a well deserved award Teacher of the Year.

12. For my mom's thirty ninth birthday May 15, my dad took her to her favorite restaurant.

13. My much loved cardinals destroyed the carefully built birdhouse that I made for them.

14. Izzy had her paws on the windowsill the windowsill of our front window watching the delivery person park at the end of our driveway.

15. We tried to get our dog his name is Steve to go swimming on vacation.

16. My rule following uncle always drives the strictly enforced speed limit 25 mph.

Underline the title or titles in each sentence that should be italicized.

17. Every week, my family and I eat ice cream and watch Blackish together.

18. We are reading Brian's Winter, by Gary Paulsen, in English class this trimester.

19. For my birthday, my grandparents took me to see The Lion King at the theater.

20. This Saturday, my friends and I are going to see the Barbie movie.

Name ____________________

Review Chapter 4

Complete the crossword puzzle about punctuation.

Across

1 Use a comma and a coordinate ______ to combine two independent clauses.

3 A question mark goes at the end of an ______ sentence.

5 Use a ______ to introduce a series of items in a sentence.

6 Titles of books, movies, TV shows, and newspapers are typically set in ______.

8 Dialogue is set off with commas and ______ marks.

9 Twenty two and eighty four both need a ______.

Down

1 Connect a dependent and independent clause with a comma and a subordinate conjunction in a ______ sentence.

2 In a letter, Dear Ty is the ______.

4 ______ are used in contractions, to form possessives, and to form plurals.

7 If the order of multiple adjectives to describe a noun can be switched, use a ______ between them.

Name ______________________________

Review Chapter 4

Correct each sentence by adding the missing punctuation.

1. We read To Kill a Mockingbird in class before watching the movie.

2. What is your favorite book turned movie Carly ____

3. Marco's Lawn Service does it all weeding, fertilizing, planting, and cutting.

4. My well intentioned grandmother bought me a book on hygiene called Guy Stuff, The Body Book for Boys.

5. I cant imagine what it must be like to live in Hawai'i how cool!

6. Yay, our class won the can collecting contest ____

7. I didnt find Lawrences backpack in the boys restroom.

8. You have twenty five minutes for the test said Mr. Brown and not a minute more.

9. Salzburg which is in Austria is the birthplace of Wolfgang Amadeus Mozart one of the greatest composers in history.

10. Wear your black rubber boots into the garden when you go out to pick tomatoes peppers and beans ____

11. My answer was no I didn't feel that a ten year old should be going to a late night movie.

12. Arlo, share your candy with your cute baby sister said my mom If you dont, shes going to start crying

Chapter 5: Usage

Chapter 5 is a quick chapter, but it covers usage of words and phrases that, if used incorrectly, can alter the intended meaning of a sentence or make sentences or passages difficult to understand. The skills covered in this chapter include dangling and misplaced modifiers, double negatives, wordiness, and redundancies.

Well-intentioned writers often commit modifier mishaps. When a writer knows what they're trying to say, it's easy for them to overlook that their modifier might be modifying the wrong words in a sentence, creating a misplaced modifier, or to even leave out words, creating dangling modifiers. Dangling and misplaced modifiers are common, but they don't have to be.

Negative words like **not** and **never** are used to change the meaning of a sentence. However, the use of double negatives is an easy mistake to make. If an author includes a double negative, the words automatically cancel each other out and, again, change the meaning of the sentence. Double negatives should be avoided, and Chapter 5 gives students practice at recognizing and correcting double negatives.

Wordiness and redundancy in writing can interrupt the flow of a sentence or passage. Sometimes wordiness can happen when a writer tries to sound more intelligent or convincing, but the use of too many non-essential words can detract from the true meaning that the writer is trying to express. Chapter 5 addresses how to avoid wordiness with straight-forward, concise writing that is meaningful and thoughtful. Redundancy can also cause a reader to stumble. The needless repetition of words or phrases usually results in writing that is too lengthy. Activities in Chapter 5 give students practice at recognizing redundant writing, and gives them opportunities to shorten sentences without altering the meaning.

Skills Checklist

- [ ] Identifying and correcting dangling modifiers
- [ ] Identifying and correcting misplaced modifiers
- [ ] Identifying and correcting double negatives
- [ ] Identifying and correcting wordiness
- [ ] Identifying and correcting redundancies

Helpful Definitions

modifier: a word or phrase that describes or gives more detail about a sentence; Example: *On my way into the city, I saw a train.*

dangling modifier: a word or phrase that modifies a word not clearly stated in the sentence; Example: *Having seen the movie, the book was better.*

misplaced modifier: a word or phrase placed awkwardly in a sentence and appears to modify the wrong word; Example: *Happy that work was over, the evening was quite relaxing.*

double negative: two negative words used together in a sentence; grammatically incorrect; Example: *Mandy couldn't hear nothing.*

wordiness: the use of too many words in a sentence or paragraph when fewer words can be used to say the same thing; Example: *Tonya lives in the vicinity of her friend Rudy.*

redundancy: an unnecessary repetition of information; Example: *Currently at this time the book is checked out.*

Name ____________________

Lesson 5.1 Dangling and Misplaced Modifiers

A **modifier** describes or gives more detail about the sentence. There are two types of incorrect modifiers.

A **dangling modifier** happens when the subject of the sentence is not stated.

Dangling modifier: At two years old, my family moved to another state.

Correct: When I was two years old, my family moved to another state.

A **misplaced modifier** happens when a modifier is not placed correctly in a sentence, and the meaning of the sentence may be unclear or even incorrect.

Misplaced modifier: Annie saw a fox on the way to the grocery store.

Correct: On her way to the grocery store, Annie saw a fox.

If the modifier in the sentence is correct, put a check mark on the line. If it is incorrect, write **DG** for dangling modifier or **MM** for misplaced modifier.

1. ______ Like most pets, the cashier told us that hamsters need good care.
2. ______ Driving around the corner, my uncle's house came into view.
3. ______ The photographer saw a scared zebra being chased by a lion.
4. ______ The meteorologist said we were going to have lightning on the TV.
5. ______ The actress wore a dress to present an award that was covered in sequins.
6. ______ Running toward the endzone, the ball was dropped to the ground.

Can you write a sentence with either a dangling or misplaced modifier? Try it!

____

____

Name ___________________________________

Lesson 5.1 Dangling and Misplaced Modifiers

The sentences have either a dangling modifier or a misplaced modifier. Rewrite each sentence to correct the modifier. You may have to add words or phrases to complete it.

1. Lindsey saw a deer skateboarding to the park.

____

2. Almost nine years old, my mom thought it was time for me to start making my bed.

____

3. After sprinting to the bus stop, the bus still pulled away without Ben.

____

4. Jacob promised to wash the dishes running out the door.

____

5. Biking over the bridge, a freighter suddenly appeared.

____

6. Swimming in the lake, the rip currents were getting worse.

____

Name ______________________________

Lesson 5.2 Double Negatives

Double negatives occur when two negative words are used in the same sentence. Negative words include *not, no, never, nobody, nowhere, nothing, barely, hardly, scarcely*, and contractions containing the word *not*. Avoid using double negatives because they are grammatically incorrect.

To correct a double negative, you can delete one of the negative words or replace it with an affirmative, or positive, word. Affirmative words are the opposite of negative words. Examples include *some, somewhere, someone, anyone, any*, and *always*.

Negative: **"Don't do anything** yet with the cookie dough," said my mom.
Double Negative: **"Don't do nothing** yet with the cookie dough," said my mom.

Negative: I **don't have any** new emails to check.
Double Negative: I **don't have no** new emails to check.

Circle the word or words in parentheses that best complete each sentence.

1. Because of the impending snowstorm, the plane couldn't go (nowhere, anywhere).
2. Sammy doesn't think that (nobody, anyone) likes going to the art museum with him.
3. Our group should have received extra time to work on our project, but we didn't get (any, none).
4. Greg could barely see (anything, nothing) in the murky lake water.
5. We couldn't find (nowhere, anywhere) to park for the parade.

Can you write a sentence with a double negative, and then write it correctly without the double negative? Try it!

____

____

____

Name ______________________________

Lesson 5.2 Double Negatives

Each sentence below contains a double negative. Rewrite the sentences to eliminate the double negatives. There may be more than one correct answer for each item.

1. My puppy won't eat none of his new puppy food.

   ____

2. Don't nobody drink the spoiled milk.

   ____

3. Iman can't hardly wait for the concert this weekend.

   ____

4. Kevin didn't care about nothing except going to the gym.

   ____

5. Because of the ice storm, we're not going nowhere tonight.

   ____

6. There wasn't nobody in line to buy tickets at 10:00.

   ____

7. I haven't never tried raw oysters.

   ____

8. Ahmad doesn't want nothing to do with his unfriendly neighbor.

   ____

Name ______________________________

Lesson 5.3 Wordiness

Wordiness is when a writer uses more words, phrases, or sentences than necessary to say what they want to say. To keep your writing clear, concise, and easy to read, you want to avoid wordiness.

Wordy: **The man who drove the bus** opened the door for us.

Not wordy: **The bus driver** opened the door for us.

Rewrite each sentence so that it isn't as wordy. Do this by eliminating words, using new words, or combining short sentences into one sentence.

1. The woman who was ringing up our groceries was very friendly.

____

2. My dentist is a friendly woman. My dentist has red hair and a nice smile.

____

3. Lola quit her job on account of the fact that it was necessary for her to be home more to help take care of her grandmother.

____

____

4. The reason Jamal chose the Strikers soccer camp was because it was inexpensive in price.

____

5. Mother's Day falls in the month of May.

____

Name ______________________________

Lesson 5.3 Wordiness

If the sentence is too wordy, rewrite a shortened version of it on the line. If it is ok as is, put a check mark before it.

1. ______ My aunt and uncle live in the vicinity of Buffalo, New York.

____

2. ______ At 3:30pm in the afternoon, a black dog that was seen by me was chasing a white dog that was seen by me.

____

3. ______ It is supposed that young children can learn how to tie their shoes around the age of four.

____

4. ______ The morning train arrived as scheduled.

____

5. ______ The announcement, which was read at the beginning of the day, told us to expect a fire drill later today.

____

6. ______ The golfer who golfs the best will win a spot on the team.

____

Explain why a paragraph or story that is too wordy might be difficult to read.

____

____

Name ______________________________

Lesson 5.4 Eliminating Redundancies

When a writer repeats himself or herself, it is called **redundancy**. To keep your writing clear and to the point, you should avoid being redundant. Think, less is more.
Avoid using long, unnecessary phrases, such as **"Due to the fact that," "In the event that,"** or **"As far as I'm concerned."**
Avoid repeating yourself with phrases like "2 am **in the morning**" or "I saw it **with my own eyes.**"
When using acronyms, don't repeat words already contained in the acronym, such as "I need to stop at the ATM **machine.**" **Machine** is already included in the acronym.

Redundant: Maya Angelou wrote an autobiography **about her life.**
(**about her life** is redundant because an autobiography is about someone's life)
Not redundant: Maya Angelou wrote an autobiography.

Cross off the redundant word(s) in each sentence. Rewrite the sentences without those words.

1. I decided to buy the make-up because I got a free gift with purchase.

____

2. It's a true fact that my dog is half Chihuahua and half Dachshund.

____

3. I stayed up until 11:30 at night last night.

____

4. The beams were shorter in length than what the carpenter needed.

____

5. My friend briefly summarized the new book.

____

6. Since nobody saw if the serve was in or out, they replayed the point again.

____

Name ______________________________

Lesson 5.4 Eliminating Redundancies

These sentences contain redundant words. Circle the words that are redundant and explain why they are not necessary to the meaning of the sentence.

1. The Pest Patrol sprayed our backyard to kill mosquitoes dead.

____

2. I was allowed to take one suitcase, so I packed only the basic essentials.

____

3. My new friend is always so happy and joyful.

____

4. I woke up at 9 am in the morning to thunderstorms.

____

5. Do you think you'll return again to the new bakery on the corner?

____

6. If the yarn is longer in length than you need, you can trim it.

____

Explain why writing sentences that are more concise is better than writing sentences that are redundant.

____

____

Name ______________________________

Review Chapter 5

On the line, write if the sentence contains a dangling modifier (**DM**) or a misplaced modifier (**MM**). Then rewrite the sentence so the modifier is correct.

1. ______ Racing ever closer toward the goalie, the puck was lost just inches from the goal.

____

2. ______ While skateboarding to the park, a fire truck went screaming by.

____

3. ______ My dog spied a raccoon glancing out the window.

____

4. ______ Our Aunt Shania said on Sunday she would call us.

____

5. ______ I saw the helicopter looking out over the lake.

____

6. ______ Upon boarding the plane, a crying baby caught my eye.

____

Rewrite the sentences so they do not contain a double negative.

7. I didn't yell at nobody.

____

8. Leila couldn't find no place to park.

____

9. I don't have no ice for the cooler.

____

10. The avocado wasn't no good anymore.

____

Name ______________________________

Review Chapter 5

Rewrite each wordy sentence using fewer words.

11. The rules of the classroom have been established for the safety of all students in the room.

____

____

12. Maleek told a deliberate lie on purpose for the purpose of getting me to believe that he had made the basketball team that he tried out for.

____

____

13. My grandma made us dinner on account of the fact that my mom had to work late and my dad was out of town on a business trip for the company he worked for.

____

____

Underline the redundant words in the sentences.

14. Carrie had new, never-before-heard rules for the game we play every Friday at 7pm in the evening.

15. Community members protested against the new dog park ordinance.

16. I declare a statement that I washed the dishes after our dinner meal.

17. Eric got cash money out of the ATM machine.

18. The suspect was surrounded on all sides by police officers.

19. I hope the bald eagle returns again to its nest.

20. We watched as the fishermen set up their shanty on the frozen ice.

Chapter 6: Word Study

In Chapter 6, students will focus on the meanings of words as they relate to other words. Exercises will show students that words not only have meaning on their own, in isolation, but that words often have relationships with other words. We start by looking at roots and affixes. Understanding that there are root words, and that these root words can have prefixes and suffixes added to them, is important in writing, reading, and conversation.

Next, we move on to synonyms (words that have the same or similar meanings) and antonyms (words that have opposite meanings). Authors frequently use synonyms to avoid using the same word multiple times. Students should strive to do this, as it adds variety and interest to writing. Antonyms are often used to show differences and contrast.

Homophones (words that sound the same but have different meanings) and homographs (words that are spelled the same but have different meanings) can be confusing to readers and writers. Writers can provide context to help readers understand the meaning of the homophone or homograph that is being used.

Connotation and denotation are important concepts to understand. Sometimes authors mean exactly what they are saying. However, there are times when authors' work has a hidden, or connotative, meaning, and readers have to "read between the lines" to truly understand the meaning of the words. It is important for writers to choose their words carefully and to avoid using a word with a connotation that doesn't align with what they are intending to say.

Similes and metaphors, allusions, and personifications are addressed in Chapter 6. These types of words and phrases allow writers to paint a vivid picture of what they are saying. Use of these figures of speech takes writing to a more advanced level and shows good command of the English language. Chapter 6 also includes analogies, which is identifying the relationship between words being compared.

Skills Checklist

- ☐ Identifying and using roots, base words, prefixes, and suffixes
- ☐ Identifying and using synonyms and antonyms
- ☐ Identifying and using homophones
- ☐ Identifying and using homographs
- ☐ Understanding and using denotations and connotations

- [ ] Identifying and writing similes and metaphors
- [ ] Understanding and completing analogies
- [ ] Understanding and identifying allusions
- [ ] Identifying and writing personifications

Helpful Definitions

root: the main part of a word; often cannot stand alone as a word; Example: *capture*

base word: a root that is a complete word; Examples: *unhappy*, *rediscover*

prefix: a word part added to the beginning of a root or base word; Examples: *re-*, *un-*, *pre-*

suffix: a word part added to the end of a root or base word; Examples: *-ful*, *-ness*, *-ly*

synonyms: words that have the same or almost the same meaning; Example: *close / near*

antonyms: words that have opposite meanings; Example: *good / bad*

homophones: words that sound the same but have different spellings and meanings; Example: *son / sun*

homographs: also called *multiple-meaning words*, words that are spelled the same but have different meanings; may also have different pronunciations; Example: *bow / bow*

denotation: a word's actual, literal meaning

connotation: a word's meaning that isn't literal but is associated with the word; may be emotional; can be seen as positive, negative, or neutral

simile: a figure of speech that compares two things using the words **like** or **as**; Example: *as big as a mountain*

metaphor: a figure of speech that compares two unlike things that are similar in some way; Example: *Bella is an angel.*

analogy: a comparison between two pairs of words; Example: *tree : leaf :: flower : petal*

allusion: an indirect mention or reference to a person, thing, or event from famous literature, history, mythology, artwork, religion, pop culture, etc.; Example: *Don't be a Scrooge.*

personification: a figure of speech that gives human characteristics to something that is not human; Example: *The stars winked at us.*

Name ______________________________

Lesson 6.1 Roots

The **root** of a word is the main part of the word. It tells the main meaning, and other word parts add to the main meaning. Often, a root cannot stand alone as a word.

The root **port** means "to carry."
The word **import** means "to carry in."
The word **portable** means "can be carried."

If an unfamiliar word contains a familiar root, knowing the meaning of the root can give you a clue to the meaning of the unfamiliar word.

A **base word** is a root that is a complete word.

The base word of **react** is act.

On the line, write an example of another word that contains the same root or base word that has been underlined. Use a dictionary if you need help.

1. verdict ______________
2. credible ______________
3. captive ______________
4. productive ______________
5. autograph ______________
6. transcribe ______________
7. construction ______________
8. tactile ______________
9. tricycle ______________
10. thermonuclear ______________
11. geothermal ______________
12. automobile ______________

Name ____________________

Lesson 6.1 Roots

Draw a line to match each root in Column A with its meaning in Column B. Use a dictionary.

Column A	Column B
1. *fort* as in *fortitude*	draw
2. *capt* as in *capture*	seize
3. *struct* as in *construct*	death
4. *graph* as in *graphic*	say
5. *flect* as in *reflection*	change
6. *pac* as in *pacify*	build
7. *mort* as in *mortal*	strength
8. *dict* as in *predict*	peace
9. *vert* as in *convert*	bend

Choose two roots from the list above. Think of a word other than the one shown for each root. Write a sentence for each one.

10. root: ____________ sentence: ____________________

____

11. root: ____________ sentence: ____________________

____

Name ______________________________

Lesson 6.2 Prefixes

Prefixes and suffixes change the meanings of root words and base words.
A **prefix** is a word part added to the beginning of a root or base word. For example, the prefix **un-** means "not" or "opposite," so **unequal** means "**not** equal."

Common prefixes and their meanings:

anti- = "against"	**antibiotic**
in-, im-, ir-, il- = "not"	**irregular, impolite**
re- = "again"	**refreeze**
de-, dis- = "not, opposite of"	**defrost, disconnect**
non- = "not"	**nonslip**
over- = "too much"	**overcook**
mis- = "wrongly"	**miscalculate**
pre- = "before"	**precut**
inter- = "between, among"	**intercoastal**

Write a word on the blank that matches each definition. The word should contain a prefix and a base word found in the definition.

1. not tied ______________________________
2. to understand wrongly ______________________________
3. act among one another ______________________________
4. not sensible ______________________________
5. load too much ______________________________
6. discover again ______________________________
7. to diagnose wrongly ______________________________
8. against freezing ______________________________
9. to register before ______________________________
10. not mature ______________________________

Name ____________________________________

Lesson 6.3 Suffixes

A **suffix** is a word part added to the end of a root or base word. Sometimes, the spelling of the root or base word changes when a suffix is added. For example, the suffix **-ness** means "state or condition of." **Happiness** means "the state or condition of being happy." The **-y** in **happy** changes to **i** before adding the suffix.

Common suffixes and their meanings:

-able = "able to"	**bendable**
-ful = "characterized by or tending to"	**playful**
-y, -ly = "characteristic of"	**angrily**
-er, -or = "one who" or "person connected with"	**dreamer**
-on, -tion, -ation, -ition = "act or process"	**animation**
-ic = "having characteristics of"	**allergic**
-less = "without"	**harmless**
-en = "made of" or "to make"	**brighten**

Read each definition below. Fill in the correct space in the crossword puzzle with a word that ends in a suffix and matches the definition. Use a dictionary if needed.

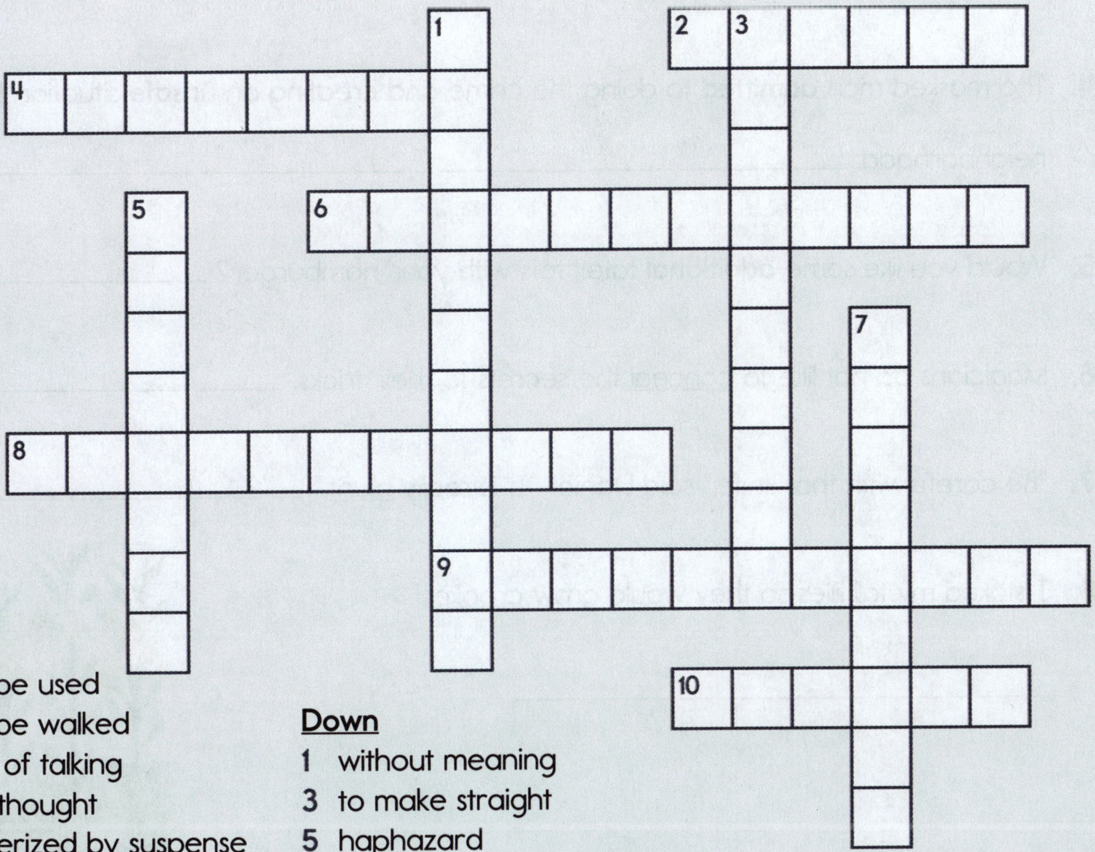

Across

2 able to be used
4 able to be walked
6 process of talking
8 without thought
9 characterized by suspense
10 being a poet

Down

1 without meaning
3 to make straight
5 haphazard
7 person who collects things

Name ______________________________

Lesson 6.4 Synonyms and Antonyms

Synonyms are words that have the same, or almost the same, meaning. Using synonyms can help you avoid repeating words and can make your writing more interesting. A thesaurus, either in a book or online, is a good source for finding synonyms.

trash / garbage **finish / complete** **noisy / loud** **talk / chat**

Antonyms are words that have opposite meanings. A dictionary, either in a book or online, is a good source for finding antonyms.

deep / shallow **good / evil** **climb / descend** **allow / forbid**

On the line, write a synonym for bold words and an antonym for underlined words.

1. I am going to **ask** for more time for my science project. ______________________

2. The Millers are always <u>late</u> for dinner parties. ______________________

3. My mom always does her yoga in the <u>morning</u>. ______________________

4. The masked man **admitted** to doing the crime and creating an **unsafe** situation for the neighborhood. ______________________ ______________________

5. Would you like some **additional** tater tots with your hamburger? ______________________

6. Magicians do not like to <u>conceal</u> the secrets to their tricks. ______________________

7. "Be careful with that knife," said Daniel. "It is really <u>blunt</u>." ______________________

8. I staked my tall lilies so they would grow <u>crooked</u>.

____

Name ____

Lesson 6.4 Synonyms and Antonyms

Draw a line to match each word in column A with its synonym in column B. Then, draw a line to match each word in column C with its antonym in column D.

A	B	C	D
1. begin	bother	10. east	captive
2. broad	untrue	11. ally	bitter
3. annoy	instructions	12. separate	ancient
4. decide	chilly	13. despair	general
5. cut	start	14. modern	west
6. cold	chop	15. sweet	enemy
7. complex	determine	16. graceful	join
8. directions	complicated	17. specific	hope
9. false	wide	18. free	clumsy

Use an online dictionary or thesaurus to find the following synonyms or antonyms.

19. an antonym for *optimism* ____________________

20. a synonym for *mistake* ____________________

21. a synonym for *reject* ____________________

22. an antonym for *generous* ____________________

Name ______________________________

Lesson 6.5 Homophones

Homophones are words that sound the same but have different spellings and different meanings. There are hundreds of homophones in the English language.

bred— to produce	*ducks*— a swimming bird	*break*— to separate into parts
bread— a food	*ducts*— a tube or pipe	*brake*— to apply pressure to stop

If you are unsure about which homophone to use, look up the meanings in a dictionary.

Circle the correct homophone(s) in each sentence.

1. Many wildfires are burning in (grease, Greece) this summer.
2. Ken's teenage children let out a (groan, grown) when he told his joke.
3. Mr. Andrews (aloud, allowed) Jess to go (to, too, two) the restroom during homeroom.
4. The stray dog had (course, coarse) fur because of its unhealthy diet.
5. "Jaxson, can you please (grate, great) the cheese for the tacos?" asked his dad.
6. Kelly (led, lead) her friends to the basement (where, wear) they could play video games.
7. The leak in the (sealing, ceiling) ruined (they're, there, their) carpet.
8. The construction crew was to (build, billed) a ramp for Mr. Henshaw's wheelchair.

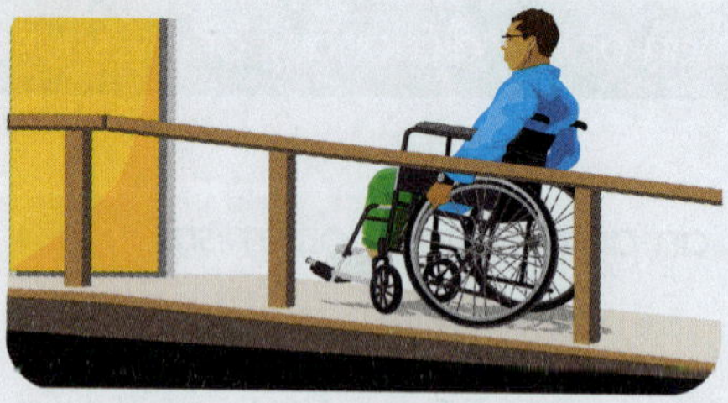

Can you write a sentence that contains one or more homophones? Try it! Circle the homophones.

____

____

Name ___________________________

Lesson 6.5 Homophones

Proofread the following dialogue. It contains multiple errors in homophones. There are 26 mistakes to correct in all.

deletes incorrect letters, words, punctuation	inserts correct letters, words, punctuation

"I have good gnus, Mom," JaLean said to her mom as she walked threw the door.

"Oh, I can't weight to here it! I've had a boring day, so I could use sum good news," her mom replied.

"On the weigh to get my hare cut, I ran into Mr. Lewis. Ewe no him. He's my English teacher from this passed year."

"Yes, I remember him," said JaLeans's mom.

"He told me that he liked the paper that I rote on Ireland sew much that he wants me to right for the school newspaper next year."

"That's exciting!" said JaLean's mom. "Dew you want two?"

"Of coarse I want two!" exclaimed JaLean. "He told me that the writers get to chews what to right about. He said last year there were articles about the whether, a local stake restaurant, rapping presents for the holidays, and even an article about our principle, Mrs. Teague."

"Sounds like a lot of fun," said her mom. "I'm glad he offered that too you."

"I feel like I one the lottery!" laughed JaLean.

Name ____________________

Lesson 6.6 Multiple-Meaning Words

Multiple-meaning words, or **homographs**, are words that are spelled the same but have different meanings. They may also sometimes have different pronunciations.

The word *tear* can mean "to rip" or it can mean "a drop of fluid from the eye."

Careful, or you'll *tear* your shirt on the nail that is sticking up.

The woman wiped a *tear* from her eye during the emotional speech.

Read each sentence below. Then, write a new sentence using a different meaning for the underlined word. Use a dictionary if you need help.

1. The kids wanted to sit up front in the bow of the boat.

   ____

2. The coach did not approve of his player's conduct on the field.

   ____

3. Please do not subject the children to your dumb jokes.

   ____

4. We set out our picnic near the bank of the river.

   ____

5. I couldn't bear to watch the mother ignoring her crying child.

   ____

6. My mom is going to contest the speeding ticket that she got.

   ____

What can help you figure out the meaning of a homograph in a sentence?

____

____

Name ______________________________

Lesson 6.6 Multiple-Meaning Words

Read each pair of definitions below the word search. Think of the multiple-meaning word that fits both the definitions and then find it in the word search puzzle. Words may be found horizontally or vertically.

b	n	o	v	e	l	c	j	w	e	s	g	l
g	a	k	c	o	t	d	m	e	p	a	r	s
p	w	a	l	c	h	e	l	n	r	o	c	n
m	a	p	t	h	a	f	i	m	o	p	e	d
v	t	o	c	g	w	e	v	i	j	o	w	a
a	c	p	k	r	o	c	k	n	e	m	i	l
n	h	w	a	s	q	t	s	o	c	s	n	c
l	r	k	s	u	s	p	e	c	t	i	d	t

1. an imperfection; to forsake a cause or nation due to a change in thought

___ ___ ___ ___ ___ ___

2. an instrument that is worn and tells time; to look at

___ ___ ___ ___ ___

3. to move back and forth; a piece of earth

___ ___ ___ ___

4. something specific to work on; to display outwardly

___ ___ ___ ___ ___ ___ ___

5. a movement of air; to wrap something around an object

___ ___ ___ ___

6. someone thought to be involved in a crime; to have doubts

___ ___ ___ ___ ___ ___ ___

7. new; a book

___ ___ ___ ___ ___

8. to be sad; a small motorbike

___ ___ ___ ___ ___

Name ________________________________

Lesson 6.7 Denotations and Connotations

A word's **denotation** is its actual, literal meaning. It is the meaning you would find if you looked the word up in a dictionary.

A word's **connotation** is the meaning associated with the word. The connotation may be more emotional or tied to an idea or feeling about the word. Connotations can be positive, negative, or neutral.

For example, the words **proud, confident, arrogant**, and **egotistical** all mean to feel good about oneself. But two of the words have a positive connotation (**proud** and **confident**) and two have a negative connotation (**arrogant** and **egotistical**).

Using the pairs of words below, write each one in the chart based on their connotation.

Positive	Neutral	Negative

smirk	smile	cop	officer
aggressive	pushy	cheap	inexpensive
slender	scrawny	sad	depressed
plain	natural	young	immature
gaze	stare	obese	overweight
smart	genius	old	vintage
chef	cook		

Name ______________________________

Lesson 6.7 Denotations and Connotations

Complete each sentence below with a word from the word bank. The word you choose should have a similar denotation but different connotation from the word in parentheses.

immature	**wild**	**liar**	**collects**
private	**stingy**	**unique**	**inquisitive**

1. I heard my mom telling my dad that our neighbors are (nosy) ____________________.
2. Kent's hobby of painting with his toes is very (bizarre) ____________________.
3. My uncle (hoards) ____________________ concert wristbands.
4. The new puppy next door certainly is (energetic) ____________________.
5. I haven't saved much money, so I'm often (frugal) ____________________ with how I spend it.
6. LeAnn claims that Jake is a (fibber) ____________________ and always making up stories.
7. My cousin, who is an introvert, is very (independent) ____________________.
8. The kid in the park was too old to be acting so (childish) ____________________.

Why is it important to choose words carefully when writing? Explain.

____

____

Name ______________________________

Lesson 6.8 Similes and Metaphors

A **simile** is a figure of speech that compares two things using the words **like** or **as**.
Antoine's angry stare directed at his sister was **as cold as ice.**
The boys' friendship fell apart once Vern realized that Jamie was **as cunning as a fox.**

A **metaphor** is a figure of speech that compares two unlike things that are similar in some way.
The marathoners' steps were a metronome, thumping a steady beat along the street.
Our dog Willie **is such a couch potato.**

On the line, write the two things that are being compared and which figure of speech is being used (simile or metaphor).

1. On the day of the party, Mr. Reinick's classroom was a zoo.

____

2. My friend Rex is a walking dictionary.

____

3. Liam stands proud and tall, like the peaks of a mountain range.

____

4. The ghost pepper is like a fire blazing in my mouth!

____

5. Our computer lab at school is filled with old dinosaurs.

____

6. Life is like a dream, I thought as I relaxed by the ocean.

____

7. The banana peel was as yellow as the sun.

____

Name ______________________________

Lesson 6.8 Similes and Metaphors

Rewrite each sentence so that it contains a simile or metaphor to make the writing more descriptive or interesting to read.

1. The lilies grew tall in the colorful garden.

____

2. The sun flooded the living room with light.

____

3. The dogs ran excitedly into the fenced-in dog park.

____

4. Thunder rumbled off in the distance for hours.

____

5. Grace's new moped was shiny and red.

____

6. The kite flew high in the air on the gentle breezes.

____

7. Grandma Jane was a petite woman who often wore a shy smile.

____

8. The commuter train rumbled into the station.

____

9. As the coyote stalked through the woods, leaves crinkled underfoot.

____

10. The edges of the roof lifted higher as the wind grew stronger.

____

Name ______________________________

Lesson 6.9 Analogies

An **analogy** is a comparison between two pairs of words. To complete an analogy, figure out how the pairs of words are related.

Forest is to **tree** as **beach** is to **sand**.
A forest consists of trees, just as a beach consists of sand.

Leap is to **jump** as **soar** is to **fly**.
Leap is a synonym for **jump**, just as **soar** is a synonym for **fly**.

Lens is to **camera** as **page** is to *book*.
A lens is part of a camera, just as a page is part of a book.

Analogies are often presented without using the phrase **is to** and the word **as**. Instead, colons are used in place of *is to*, and two colons are used in place of *as* to separate the pairs being compared.

Movie is to **DVD** as **album** is to **CD**.
movie : DVD : : album : CD

Circle the letter of the word that best completes each analogy.

1. tablecloth : table : : hat : ______________

a. closet **b.** head **c.** fold **d.** arm

2. fish : ______________ : : tree : bark

a. ocean **b.** scales **c.** water **d.** fin

3. ______________ : pen : : paint : brush

a. artist **b.** pencil **c.** paper **d.** ink

4. hamster : wheel : : ______________ : track

a. wrestler **b.** swimmer **c.** runner **d.** gerbil

5. blueberries : muffins : : chocolate chips : ______________

a. milk **b.** eggs **c.** cookies **d.** plate

6. puppy : dog : : bunny : ______________

a. rabbit **b.** fox **c.** bunnies **d.** fur

Name ________________________________

Lesson 6.9 Analogies

Write a word on the line that completes each analogy.

1. *Phoenix* is to *Arizona* as ____________________ is to *California*.

2. *Pod* is to *dolphins* as *school* is to ____________________.

3. *Thanksgiving* is to ____________________ as *Juneteenth* is to *June*.

4. *Aunt* is to *ant* as *die* is to ____________________.

5. *Salad* is to *tomato* as *orchestra* is to ____________________.

6. *Wet* is to ____________________ as *sunny* is to *cloudy*.

7. *Ball* is to *soccer* as *puck* is to ____________________.

8. *Scale* is to *weight* as ____________________ is to *temperature*.

Follow the directions to write your own analogies. Use the examples on this page and the previous page for help if needed.

9. Write an analogy in which the words are antonyms (like #6 above).

____

____

10. Write an analogy that shows a part-to-whole relationship (like #5 above).

____

____

Name ______________________________

Lesson 6.10 Allusions

An **allusion** is where the writer indirectly mentions or references a person, thing, or event. It can be from famous literature, history, mythology, artwork, religion, pop culture, and more. It is assumed that the reader is familiar with the topic being alluded to.

Mike is the **pied piper** of our neighborhood.

Mikhail hit the bench press like he was **the Incredible Hulk**.

Underline the allusion in each sentence.

1. The man who stopped to help Maggie change her flat tire was her Prince Charming.
2. The latest drama in Marcus's family is much ado about nothing.
3. My mom is worried that her new boss is a Trojan horse, so she is looking for a new job.
4. It was easy to trick Tina because she was as gullible as Alice.
5. Hot fudge sundaes are Kelli's kryptonite.
6. Ollie had cried wolf one too many times, so no one believed him.
7. Moving the large rocks out of the water and back up onto the seawall was a Herculean task for the teenage boys.
8. Levi thinks he's the Tiger Woods of miniature golf.

Explain why you might want to include allusions in your writing.

____

____

Name ______________________________

Lesson 6.10 Allusions

Underline the allusion in each sentence. Use an online resource to identify what the allusion is referring to. Write the topic or source of the allusion on the line.

Example: Trent hit one three-point shot during our pick-up game and now he thinks he's LeBron James.

Source/topic: basketball player, plays for the Los Angeles Lakers

1. I make mistakes too; I'm no Mother Teresa.

Source/topic: ______________________________

2. The mayor took to the podium with the confidence of Cicero.

Source/topic: ______________________________

3. My dad seems to carry the weight of the world on his shoulders.

Source/topic: ______________________________

4. Len looked adoringly at Meg and said, "I want to be Romeo to your Juliet."

Source/topic: ______________________________

5. Stella wanted to click her heels and be back home.

Source/topic: ______________________________

6. Chaz, who soared above his basketball teammates, was a Titan.

Source/topic: ______________________________

Name ____

Lesson 6.11 Personification

Personification is a figure of speech that gives human characteristics to something that is not human.

The raindrops slid lazily down the window panes.
The book called out to me from the bookshelf.
Lightning danced across the sky.

Underline the personification in each sentence.

1. The cherry fudge pie was calling my name.

2. When the cool water touched my feet, it soothed my sunburn.

3. It's true that time flies when you're having fun.

4. My annoying alarm clock yells at me every morning when it goes off.

5. The brakes on Amelio's car whined as he slowly came to a stop.

6. The strip in Las Vegas is alive and kicking 24/7.

7. The winds howled as they grew stronger with each gust.

8. My thirsty flowers were wilting in the summer heat.

9. The scary story jumped off the page!

10. The old tree groaned as the strong wind pushed on it.

11. The engine roared to life when he turned the key in the ignition.

12. The warm blanket hugged my body.

Name ______________________________

Lesson 6.11 Personification

Write sentences that contain a personification. Use the topics given.

1. a hurricane ______________________________

____

2. a candle ______________________________

____

3. a cheesecake ______________________________

____

4. a flagpole ______________________________

____

5. a bowling ball ______________________________

____

6. a haunted house ______________________________

____

Explain why it can be good to include personifcation in your writing.

____

____

Name ______________________________

Review Chapter 6

Write a word using each root.

1. dict ______________________ **2.** struct ______________________

For each prefix or suffix, locate its meaning in the box. Write the meaning on the first line, and then write an example of a word that uses the prefix or suffix on the second line.

wrongly	**one who**	**characterized by or tending to**
not or opposite of	**again**	**without**

3. -er ______________________ ______________________

4. re- ______________________ ______________________

5. -ful ______________________ ______________________

6. mis- ______________________ ______________________

7. -less ______________________ ______________________

8. dis- ______________________ ______________________

For each word, write the letter of either its synonym or antonym on the line.

9. ______ giving a. special

10. ______ unique b. nervous

11. ______ confident c. selfish

12. ______ agreeable d. drape

13. ______ curtain e. argumentative

14. ______ anxious f. insecure

Name ______________________________

Review Chapter 6

Circle the word in parentheses that best completes each analogy.

15. arctic : (shark, polar bear) : : woods : owl

16. Akron : Ohio : : Seattle : (Montana, Washington)

17. itching : scratching : : tired : (yelling, yawning)

18. Valentine's Day : (February, April) : : Labor Day : September

Read each definition. Choose the correct homophone from the word bank and write it on the line.

dense	**serial**	**dents**	**cereal**
muscle	**cymbal**	**mussel**	**symbol**

19. ____________________ breakfast food eaten with milk

20. ____________________ a percussion instrument made of two metal plates that are clapped together

21. ____________________ thick; crowded together

22. ____________________ organ in the body that produces movement

Identify the underlined words as a simile (S), metaphor (M), allusion (A), or personification (P).

23. Marlee's voice is <u>music to my ears</u>. ______

24. The big city is <u>calling my name</u>. ______

25. My grandma is <u>as busy as a bee</u> in her garden. ______

26. Fanny's <u>mysterious smile reminds me of the Mona Lisa's</u>. ______

Name ______________________________

Learning Checkpoint Chapters 4–6

Fill in the blanks.

1. An ______________ sentence asks a question.

2. ______________ and ______________ sentences end with a period.

3. Exclamation points can be used at the end of ______________ or ______________ sentences.

Add the correct ending punctuation to the sentences.

4. Do you know the date of your orchestra concert ___

5. Grab the rope ___

6. I am getting hot lunch today at school ___

7. I am so excited for the concert this weekend ___

Add commas where they are needed.

8. "Your son is a responsible conscientious boy," said Mr. Thalen.

9. After Keisha ate some breakfast she felt much better.

10. Rowan don't forget to ask your teacher about your incorrect quiz grade.

11. Marlee was stopping at the post office the grocery store and the bank while she was out.

12. The landscape was filled with tall glorious sunflowers for as far as the eye could see.

13. I didn't stretch before running and tonight my legs are sore.

14. The top three winners of the annual dog show were the Bloodhound the Standard Poodle and the Wire Fox Terrier.

Name ______________________________

Learning Checkpoint Chapters 4–6

Semicolons, colons, quotation marks, apostrophes, and hyphens are missing from these sentences. Rewrite each sentence with the missing punctuation added in.

15. The boys hockey team is going to the state finals it'll be an amazing game.

____

16. Keisha said Mrs. Brooks youre the runner up of the weekly math contest!

____

17. Bryn couldnt fit these items in her closet her saxophone her boots and her folded up chair.

____

18. I have twenty five dollars for the book fair I want to buy these items a mystery book, a graphic novel, and a keychain.

____

19. Your science teacher said, Olive is a great leader in our class, said her mom at dinner.

____

20. My grandpa turned the wrong way down a one way street he did a U turn so we wouldnt be going the wrong way.

____

____

Name ______________________________

Learning Checkpoint Chapters 4–6

Rewrite these sentences so they do not contain a dangling or misplaced modifier.

21. Laughing loudly, the movie ended.

____

22. I served Deion's birthday cake to the kids on paper plates.

____

23. Looking out over Lake Michigan, a big storm was brewing.

____

24. Jogging over the bridge, the sun was setting.

____

Circle the word in parentheses that completes the sentence without creating a double negative.

25. Evian hasn't seen (neither, either) the garbage or recycle truck come this morning.

26. Ronny's moped didn't have (any, no) gas left in the tank.

27. The seagulls couldn't find (nowhere, anywhere) to land.

Name ____________________

Learning Checkpoint Chapters 4–6

Write the prefix, root word, and suffix for each word below.

	Prefix	Root	Suffix
28. impassable	______	______	______
29. enjoyable	______	______	______
30. impatiently	______	______	______
31. disrespectful	______	______	______
32. miscommunication	______	______	______

Write a synonym or antonym for each underlined word.

33. This summer, Jonah and Christian <u>built</u> a treehouse.

Synonym: ____________________

34. Marylou liked the look of the <u>modern</u> desk.

Antonym: ____________________

35. The new deck had <u>straight</u> spindles.

Antonym: ____________________

36. The hurricane <u>wrecked</u> the Sanchez's beachside home.

Synonym: ____________________

Name ______________________________

Learning Checkpoint Chapters 4–6

Circle the correct homophone that makes sense in the sentence.

37. (Some, Sum) of my favorite hobbies are swimming, drawing, and reading.

38. DeShaun's team (one, won) the Little League World Series!

39. Our neighbor's condo is for (sail, sale).

40. The black dog's (tale, tail) had some white on it.

Write two sentences for each homograph. Use a different meaning for each homograph.

41. wind ______________________________

wind ______________________________

42. produce ______________________________

produce ______________________________

Underline the simile or metaphor. On the line write whether it is a simile (S) or metaphor (M).

43. My youth group leader has a heart of gold. ______

44. Harrison's sunburned face was as red as a lobster. ______

45. This traffic jam is a pain in the neck. ______

46. The stale bagel was as hard as a rock. ______

Name ______________________________

Learning Checkpoint Chapters 4–6

Circle the letter of the word that completes each analogy.

47. broccoli : green :: raspberry : ____________

a. sweet **b.** red **c.** fruit **d.** juicy

48. stars : galaxy :: ____________ : foot

a. shoe **b.** stand **c.** toes **d.** body

49. cat : ____________ :: dog : canine

a. feline **b.** claws **c.** scratch **d.** fur

50. ____________ : wool :: chicken : egg

a. goat **b.** sweater **c.** sheep **d.** socks

Underline the allusion (A) or personification (P) in each sentence. Write on the line which type it is.

51. The bed groaned as Milo sank into it. ______

52. Don't act like a Scrooge! ______

53. The sun played hide and seek behind the clouds. ______

54. French fries are my Achilles' heel. ______

Write a personification for each topic below.

55. car ____

56. waves ____

Name ____

Final Test

Label the underlined noun as either common, proper, collective, or abstract.

1. My friendship with Darlene is very important to me. ________________

2. The swarm of bees chased Rex down the hill. ________________

3. Mount Fuji is an active volcano in Japan. ________________

4. The chain on Chevy's bicycle keeps falling off. ________________

5. The magician picked a participant from the audience. ________________

6. The six-year-old boy showed a lot of maturity when he donated his toys. ________________

Write the possessive form of each bold noun.

7. two **houses** driveways ________________ driveways

8. multiple **kids** artwork ________________ artwork

9. one **trucks** tires ________________ tires

10. six **mens** shirts ________________ shirts

Underline the intensive or reflexive pronoun in each sentence.

11. The bear scratched itself against the tree.

12. I myself prefer lemonade to tea.

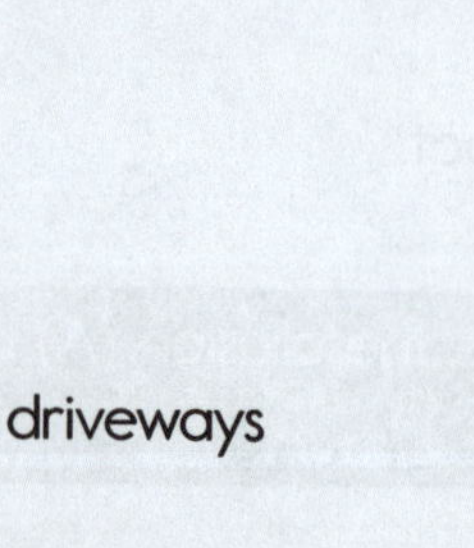

Name ______________________________

Final Test

Circle the verb that agrees with the subject.

13. Both Lin and Mason ______________ chocolate milk. (prefer, prefers)

14. Neither the coach nor his players ______________ opponents with bad sportsmanship. (like, likes)

15. The mice ______________ away whenever they hear footsteps. (scurry, scurries)

16. Either my grandparents or my mom ______________ our dog every day. (walk, walks)

17. Khalil ______________ a mile a minute! (talk, talks)

18. Maxwell and Jayla ______________ the trombone in band. (play, plays)

Write the past tense of each irregular verb.

19. sleep ______________

20. understand ______________

21. tell ______________

22. think ______________

Name ___________________________________

Final Test

Choose a comparative or superlative adjective from the word bank that correctly completes each sentence.

stronger	quieter	more beautiful	more rambunctious
strongest	quietest	most beautiful	most rambunctious

23. My big brother, who lifts weights every day, is the ______________________ person I know.

24. Our new puppy is ______________________ than our senior dog.

25. Lucille is the ______________________ girl in our class.

26. The Jamison's garden is the ______________________ one I've ever seen.

Circle the adverb, intensifier, or conjunction in each sentence.

27. The burglar moved quietly through the house.

28. Both Rinaldo and Lisa went to the splash park.

29. Mya carefully set the glass bottle in the recycling bin.

30. The ocean water around Miami is extremely hot this summer.

31. Since this room is really dark, we'll paint it a lighter color.

32. The question my neighbor asked me was rather strange.

Name ______________________________

Final Test

Create simple, compound, and complex sentences by combining a phrase or sentence from each column. Draw a line to connect them.

33. Gene went to camp,	**a.** all got treats.
34. You should wash your car	**b.** because the lawn mower was loud.
35. Are you a fan of Daniel Craig,	**c.** but he came home after two days.
36. The dogs and cats in the shelter	**d.** before your road trip.
37. Seth closed his bedroom window	**e.** so he is going to retake it.
38. Ivan failed his algebra test,	**f.** who plays 007 in James Bond movies?

On the line, write whether the bold words are an adjective (ADJ) or adverb (ADV) clause.

39. The Lismans drive a car **that is too small for their tall family.** __________

40. **While the sun is out,** I am going to plant some flowers. __________

41. We will plan our weekend **once we see what the weather will be like.** __________

42. Ms. Carinelli, **who is the leasing manager**, showed us the apartment we could rent. __________

Name ____________________

Final Test

If the sentence is capitalized correctly, write C on the line. If it is incorrect, write I on the line.

43. ______ "will you go to the dance with me, Gwen?" Asked Emmett.

44. ______ "Those two limbs," said my dad as he pointed at the tree, "are dead."

45. ______ "My laptop is broken," said Blaine. "it'll be a week before it's fixed."

Put the proofreading mark of three small lines underneath the letters that should be capitalized.

46. The affordable care act was signed into law in 2010 by president Barack Obama.

47. I want to visit the louvre museum in paris, france someday.

48. Alex's aunt works for the Michigan department of natural resources.

49. The Battle of Gettysburg took place in 1863 during the civil war.

50. Byron's family is taking a trip to the east coast.

51. Quarterback Aaron Rodgers left the green bay packers for the new york jets.

52. I like to make sandwiches on french bread.

Name ______________________________

Final Test

Circle the end mark that correctly completes each sentence.

53. Did you know that astronauts are taller when they return to Earth (. ? !)

54. The lack of gravity in outer space allows their spines to stretch out (. ? !)

55. Wow, that is so cool (. ? !)

56. Tell me more (. ? !)

Circle the letter of the sentence that has correctly placed commas.

57. **a.** The man with thick, black eyebrows looked mysterious.

b. The man with thick black eyebrows looked mysterious.

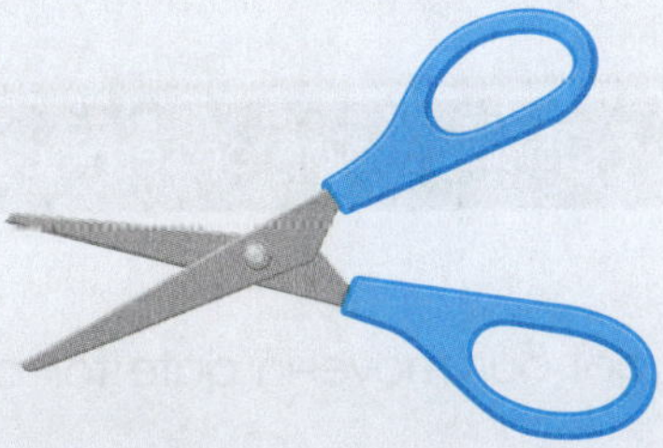

58. **a.** Can you please hand me the scissors Samia?

b. Can you please hand me the scissors, Samia?

59. **a.** The soon-to-be mother liked the names of Riley, Rashad, and Ruby for her baby.

b. The soon-to-be mother liked the names of Riley Rashad and Ruby for her baby.

60. **a.** My dad shrunk my red cotton sweater in the dryer.

b. My dad shrunk my red, cotton sweater in the dryer.

61. **a.** For Theo's week at camp, he packed a sleeping bag, clothes, and a fan.

b. For Theo's week at camp he packed a sleeping bag clothes and a fan.

62. **a.** I've told you a thousand times, Taron, to write your thank-you notes.

b. I've told you a thousand times Taron to write your thank-you notes.

Name ______________________________

Final Test

These sentences are missing commas. Write on the line how many commas are missing. Add the commas where they belong.

63. "Let's ride our bikes to the park" said Miquel "and then go get ice cream." ______

64. Because of the wildfire smoke in the air the fireworks have been canceled. ______

65. "You should think about becoming a web developer" said my mom. ______

66. If you have time swing by Sam's house to pick up your bag books and coat. ______

67. My uncle said he is coming to visit this summer and I can't wait to see him. ______

Circle whether a colon or semicolon should be used on the line in the sentence.

68. We got our move-in date for our apartment ___ it is later than we thought. (: ;)

69. I picked up these appliances for our kitchen ___ a toaster, an air fryer, a blender, and a crockpot. (: ;)

70. We're excited about our new apartment ___ it is bigger than our current one. (: ;)

71. The apartment complex has the following ___ a pool, a gym, a playground, and a dog park. (: ;)

72. Our lease is for one year ___ I hope we stay longer. (: ;)

Name ____________________________

Final Test

These sentences are missing apostrophes. Circle the words in each sentence that need an apostrophe.

73. I couldnt believe how loud the thunder was as the clouds moved in.

74. Ill be on a mission trip on my parents anniversary this year.

75. The teachers and students cheers could be heard down the hall.

76. Ive never seen a tail as crooked as Kais dogs tail.

Add hyphens where they are needed in each sentence.

77. It is a toss up as to which ridiculously cute puppy my friend's family chooses.

78. Since we were just picking up my sister at the airport, we parked in short term parking.

79. Even though I spent twenty five dollars, I came home from the carnival empty handed.

80. When my brother marries Shelby, she'll be my new sister in law.

Underline the words that should appear in italics.

81. My friend who loves art told me to check out Hey, Kiddo from the library.

82. Every night my dad tries to answer the questions on Jeopardy!

Name ______________________________

Final Test

Rewrite each sentence so it does not include a dangling or misplaced modifier, a double negative, or redundant words.

83. The grandfather clock chimed at twelve midnight.

____

84. Wren saw an owl on the way to play practice.

____

85. The teacher did not want to repeat her directions again.

____

86. Don't put no mayonnaise on my turkey sandwich.

____

87. At just one month old, Casey's family got a new dog.

____

88. Because of the big ice storm, we won't never make it out of town.

____

Name ______________________________

Final Test

Complete each sentence with the correct word from the word bank.

revisit	**unmotivated**	**playful**	**wisely**
misbehave	**kindness**	**reckless**	**preview**

89. "Do not ______________________ for your babysitter," warned our mom.

90. The nurse showed ______________________ to her dying patient.

91. The ______________________ puppy did zoomies in our backyard.

92. "We'll ______________________ this topic next week," said our teacher.

93. The ______________________ driver had his license taken away.

94. The ______________________ for the new action movie was long.

95. The ______________________ athlete skipped practice all the time.

96. My mom ______________________ packed an umbrella for our trip to Seattle.

Complete the sentences.

97. Synonyms are words that ______________________________________.

98. Antonyms are words that ______________________________________.

Name ______________________________

Final Test

Circle the correct homophone in each sentence.

99. When Caleb was (groan, grown), he moved out of his parents' house.

100. Yuri will be in trouble if he (breaks, brakes) anything at my house.

101. Why did you (bye, by, buy) this sequined jacket?

102. My uncle's favorite song is "Give (Piece, Peace) a Chance" by John Lennon.

Write the definition of the homograph as it is used in the sentence.

103. My parents do not <u>permit</u> me to have a cell phone. ______________________

104. There was a pile of <u>bark</u> at the foot of the tree. ______________________

Underline the simile or metaphor in each sentence. Circle if it is a simile (S) or a metaphor (M).

105. The snow is a white blanket covering our roof. **(S, M)**

106. My hands were as cold as ice after skiing for four hours. **(S, M)**

107. Waking up every morning at 5:00, my dad is an early bird. **(S, M)**

108. Travon was as proud as a peacock when he got an A on his test. **(S, M)**

Name ______________________________

Final Test

Circle the letter of the word that best completes each analogy.

109. Tampa : ____________ :: Detroit : Michigan

a. Missouri **b.** United States **c.** North America **d.** Florida

110. octopus : ocean :: sloth : ____________

a. river **b.** desert **c.** rainforest **d.** lake

111. spoke : ____________ :: string : violin

a. handlebar **b.** wheel **c.** ride **d.** instrument

112. ____________ : cotton :: tire : rubber

a. field **b.** car **c.** sweater **d.** fabric

Circle whether the underlined phrase is an allusion (A) or a personification (P).

113. The fascinating story jumped off the page. (A, P)

114. You're a regular Einstein, Jermaine. (A, P)

115. I may spook easily, but I'm no cowardly lion. (A, P)

116. The sunlight danced on the surface of the Atlantic Ocean. (A, P)

Answer Key

AWV: Answers will vary
E: Answers to the Enrichment question

Lesson 1.1, page 8

1. United States, country, world **2.** Atlantic Ocean, east, Pacific Ocean, west **3.** Canada, Mexico, countries, United States **4.** bald eagle, bird, United States **5.** ranges, United States, Rocky Mountains, Appalachian Mountains **6.** place, country, Earth, Death Valley
E: AWV

Lesson 1.1, page 9

1. Every Winter we visit my Grandpa in Sarasota, florida.
2. We leave around christmas and stay until new Year's Day.
3. Our favorite Thing to do with Him is swim in the gulf of Mexico.
4. We take our Fishing poles to siesta key to try to catch Striped fish.
5. We always have to eat Shrimp at suzi's Shrimp Shack before we come home.

6. – 10. AWV

Lesson 1.2, page 10

1. bunch **2.** bouquet **3.** choir **4.** galaxy **5.** deck **6.** swarm **7.** team **8.** crowd **9.** pair **10.** fleet **11.** range

Lesson 1.2, page 11

1. is, C **2.** cheers, C **3.** was, A **4.** was, A **5.** has, C **6.** prepares, C
E: AWV

Lesson 1.3, page 12

1. woman's **2.** horses' **3.** cherries' **4.** neighbor's **5.** teams' **6.** dragonfly's

Lesson 1.3, page 13

1. PL **2.** PP **3.** PL **4.** PP **5.** PL **6.** PP **7.** PL **8.** PP **9.** SP **10.** SP **11. - 13.** AWV

Lesson 1.4, page 14

1. SailGP, an extreme sailboat race, is thrilling to watch.
2. The FIFA World Cup, which started in 1930, is watched by millions every year.
3. The Cricket World Cup, played once every four years, started in England.
4. Wimbledon, the most prestigious tennis tournament in the world, is played on grass courts.
5. The Tour de France, held in France and neighboring countries, is 23 days of cycling.
6. The Summer Olympics, held every four years, has over 300 sporting events.
7. It is believed that rugby, a game that combines football and soccer, originated in England.
8. The Daytona 500, which is 500 miles long, is 200 laps around the track.

E: Appositives add more information about a topic and can help with comprehension and understanding.

Lesson 1.4, page 15

1. - 6. AWV. Answers should fit these descriptions: **1.** needs appositive to describe Maria or Ellie **2.** needs appositive to describe side dish or menu **3.** needs appositive to describe Mr. Baumgarten or test **4.** needs appositive to describe Chloe or owner **5.** needs appositive to describe Ronald Reagan or California **6.** needs appositive to describe my aunt and I or Wicked **7.** Burlington, the largest city in Vermont, is on Lake Champlain. **8.** Mrs. Smithe, a loving teacher, is retiring at the end of the year.

Lesson 1.5, page 16

1. PP **2.** SP **3.** OP **4.** SP **5.** OP **6.** PP

Lesson 1.5, page 17

1. b **2.** a **3.** b **4.** a **5.** c **6.** c

Lesson 1.6, page 18

1. that I threw **2.** whom I like **3.** whose car was hit **4.** that was going to close **5.** which is in Virginia **6.** who was wearing a baseball hat **7.** which live in the rainforest **8.** whose ball went into the water. E: A relative pronoun clause adds more information about the subject of a sentence.

Lesson 1.6, page 19

1. that **2.** which **3.** that **4.** that **5.** Who **6.** whom **7.** who **8.** whom

Lesson 1.7, page 20

1. myself **2.** himself/herself **3.** yourselves **4.** himself **5.** themselves **6.** himself/herself **7.** ourselves **8.** myself

Lesson 1.7, page 21

1. Keisha **2.** brother and sister **3.** Lamonte **4.** Myla **5.** garage **6.** Murio family **7.** you **8.** I'm; E: AWV

Lesson 1.8, page 22

1. everyone **2.** anything **3.** no one **4.** Somebody **5.** others **6.** None

Lesson 1.8, page 23

1. cleans, everyone **2.** was, All **3.** is, Nothing **4.** are, Both **5.** likes, Somebody, **6.** has, Everyone **7.** disagrees, anybody **8.** gives, Either;
E: AWV

Lesson 1.9, page 24

1. A cartoonist must practice every day if he/she wants to get better. **2.** Our black and white poodle was the spitting image of its parents. **3.** Steven and Linh asked us if we wanted to go swimming with them. **4.** A police officer helped me with my flat tire, and he/she showed me how to do it myself it if happens again. **5.** A good fisherman will wait quietly until he/she feels a tug on the line. **6.** Most kids understand that eating healthy is good for them.

Lesson 1.9, page 25

1. they **2.** we **3.** they **4.** they **5.** her **6.** it **7.** they **8.** it **9.** them **10.** they E: If pronouns do not agree, it can cause confusion for the reader.

Review Lessons 1.1–1.9, pages 26-27

1. My family c is moving to Beaverton b, Oregon, so my mom can work for Nike b.
2. One of Andre's b favorite memories of his childhood d is visiting relatives a in Italy b and being part of a cooking class c where he learned to make lasagna a.
3. When we went to the Screamin' Coasters Amusement Park b last August b, my mom could see the excitement d and fear d on our faces when we walked into the park.
4. For our camping trip a, we packed a tent, a deck c of cards, fishing poles, raincoats, and a pair c of pie irons.

In the sentences below, circle singular possessives, underline plurals, and underline plural possessives twice.

5. Mr. Meyer's students are entering their art pieces in a citywide art contest.
6. The students' parents will drive them to the park in the city.
7. RayAnne's piece, a rendering of the city skyline, took her two weeks to draw.
8. The Lehman twins' portrait of a stray dog won first place.

Answer Key

E: sentence 7 contains the appositive **9.** they **10.** myself **11.** they **12.** their **13.** herself **14.** I, we **15.** handles **16.** them **17.** himself **18.** PP **19.** IP **20.** SP **21.** OP **22.** PP **23.** IP **24.** PP

Lesson 1.10, page 28

AWV. Possible answers are shown.

1. shone **2.** thought **3.** will collect **4.** will come **5.** wrote **6.** heard **7.** need **8.** built

Lesson 1.10, page 29

1. learning **2.** live, called **3.** read, write **4.** enjoy **5.** expect, live **6.** share **7.** read **8.** enjoyed **9.** know **10.** hope, visit; E: AWV

Lesson 1.11, page 30

1. runs **2.** travels **3.** tire **4.** cheer **5.** like **6.** works **7.** have **8.** wears

Lesson 1.11, page 31

1. Tasha and her friends are going camping. **2.** Tasha spends all morning cleaning the camper to get it ready. **3.** She vacuums the floors and wipes the counters. **4.** An hour before they leave, Natalia and Shay come over. **5.** They pack their overnight bags in the back of Tasha's car. **6.** Then Seth arrives and tosses his pillow and sleeping bag into the car. **7.** He squeezes his guitar against the roof of the car. **9.** Tasha closes the trunk and they drive away. E: A subject and verb must both be singular, or they must both be plural.

Lesson 1.12, page 32

1. The airplane rumbled loudly as it flew overhead.
2. Neyla tasted the sauce in the red squirt bottle.
3. Kody voted in the last election.
4. Miguel told me a joke that wasn't funny.
5. Edwardo remained in the hospital overnight after his surgery.
6. Oscar painted a scene on his new canvas.

E: AWV

Lesson 1.12, page 33

Example: I Tia **eats** dinner at 7:00 every night.
Tia eats quickly if she has basketball practice.

AWV. Some possible answers are below.

1. I Caitlyn **walks** up and down the beach looking for dolphins.
   Caitlyn walks a 5K race every year.
2. I The puppies **played** fetch at the park all afternoon.
   The puppies play every day.
3. I Even though she's taken just one class, Bella **sculpts** artfully.
   Even though she's taken just one class, Bella sculpts beautiful statues.
4. I The birds **bathed** playfully in the overflowing birdbath.
   The birds bathed their tiny bodies in the birdbath.
5. I The smell of the rotten eggs **spoiled** the picnic.
   The picnic was spoiled because of the rotten eggs.
6. I Neil **studied** every night for a week for his final exam.
   Neil studied his notes every night for a week for his final exam.

7.-10. AWV

Lesson 1.13, page 34

1. was (LV) **2.** had (HV) **3.** seem (LV) **4.** had (HV) **5.** was (LV) **6.** seems (LV), have (HV) **7.** had (HV) **8.** have (HV)

Lesson 1.13, page 35

is, seem, will, can, will, will, may, have, will, is, appears, are, will; E: AWV

Lesson 1.14, page 36

1. To write (I) **2.** wagging (P) **3.** to swim (I) **4.** to say (I) **5.** Growing (G) **6.** hanging (P)

Lesson 1.14, page 37

1. Hiking, gerund **2.** hiking, participle **3.** to run, infinitive **4.** Swimming, gerund **5.** to swim, infinitive **6.** swimming, gerund; E: AWV

Lesson 1.15, page 38

1. Cheers fill the theater as the movie ends. **2.** Historical fiction novels will line the bookshelves in our living room. **3.** Painting supplies were delivered to the classroom today. **4.** The woodpecker pecks at the tree trunk to find bugs. **5.** The photograph will look amazing in that new frame!

Lesson 1.15, page 39

Yesterday, our class ~~will visit~~ visited an outdoor wildlife center. After we all ~~taked~~ took our seats in the main lobby, the director, Mr. Langford, ~~will welcome~~ welcomed us and told us about what we'd be doing during our visit. He introduced us to some reptiles, amphibians, and birds of prey that we could possibly ~~saw~~ see as we ~~took~~ take our tour on the many acres of open land.

While walking near ponds and down trails, we keeped our eyes open for signs of life. We each had a notebook in which to ~~keep~~ kept notes about what we ~~seen~~ saw, including bugs, frogs, salamanders, snakes, owls, eagles, certain flowers and plants, and more. Each group leader will ~~have~~ had a net they could use to carefully ~~scooped~~ scoop up small creatures if we spotted some. This ~~will allow~~ allowed us to examine them more closely before putting them back into their habitat. Once back at the learning center, we all ~~will share~~ shared what we ~~founded~~ found and learned during our outdoor adventure.

Before we ~~leaved~~ left to go back to school, Mr. Langford ~~will tell~~ told us about the mission of the outdoor wildlife center. It raises money and awareness about outdoor education and conservation. The program ~~hoped~~ hopes to help protect and ~~restores~~ restore natural habitats.

Lesson 1.16, page 40

1. is drinking (present) **2.** are growing (present) **3.** were willing (past) **4.** is washing (present) **5.** was photographing (past) **6.** were listening (past) **7.** are hooting (present) **8.** is mashing (present)

Answer Key

Lesson 1.16, page 41

Ms. Amendo had a dog named Buster. One day while trying to work from home, Buster was trying to distract her so she would play with him. Every chance he could get he was squeaking his toy behind her chair. She was ignoring him the best she could, but he was biting his toy harder and harder so it would squeak louder. She finally turned around to scold him, but within seconds she was laughing because he had bitten the toy so hard, all the stuffing had exploded out of it. Buster had his head resting on the toy and was pouting because he had ruined it. Now Ms. Amendo could get some work done.

But just when she thought all was quiet, Ms. Amendo heard hissing. Buster had found the cat, Whiskers, and was now bothering her. Whiskers was hissing at Buster from high up on the back of a chair. Buster was taunting Whiskers by nipping at the end of her tail that was hanging down from the chair. Whiskers was pawing at Buster's head while hissing and looking very annoyed. Did that stop Buster? Nope! While Whiskers was trying to tell Buster to leave her alone, Buster lunged at Whiskers and Whiskers sprung from the chair to the curtain. She was grabbing onto it with her sharp claws. The curtain and the rod came crashing down to the floor, and Whiskers sprung underneath the couch for protection. With all the commotion, Ms. Amendo was working from home, but not getting much done.

Lesson 1.17, page 42

1. PRP **2.** PP **3.** FP **4.** PP **5.** FP **6.** FP

Lesson 1.17, page 43

1. have asked **2.** had talked **3.** will have baked **4.** had earned **5.** has lived **6.** had finished **7.** will have built **8.** had washed; E: AWV

Review Lessons 1.10–1.17, pages 44–45

1. swam **2.** was **3.** feels **4.** called **5.** has **6.** drifted **7.** taste **8.** rode **9.** passed **10.** rode **11.** hissed **12.** painted **13.** waves **14.** clangs **15.** make **16.** are **17.** a **18.** b **19.** b **20.** c **21.** a **22.** c **23.** The children are sleeping in the loft. **24.** Dolphins were following the tourist boats. **25.** When her friends came over, Lucy was eating lunch. **26.** Ally is visiting her aunt and uncle next month.

Lesson 1.18, page 46

1. The crunchy chips were a perfect choice with my Caesar salad.
2. Easter eggs are usually dyed in pastel colors.
3. The molecules appeared large through the microscope.
4. Alexander grew weary as midnight approached.
5. Alaskan salmon is a very healthy fish to eat.
6. The air smelled smoky and looked hazy.
7. At the busy beach, I ran through the hot sand to get to the cool water.
8. My mom and I took Italian cooking classes at the community center.

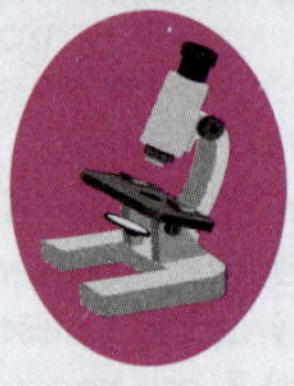

Lesson 1.18, page 47

AWV

Lesson 1.19, page 48

1. fastest **2.** windier **3.** driest **4.** busiest **5.** funniest **6.** difficult **7.** prettier **8.** dangerous

Lesson 1.19, page 49

1. noisier **2.** sicker **3.** hottest **4.** Silliest **5.** deeper **6.** most common **7.** more damaging **8.** more compassionate; E: AWV

Lesson 1.20, page 50

1. The mountain roads were extremely curvy.
2. The raspberries were rather fragile, so we picked them gently.
3. The student nervously raised her hand to answer the question.
4. Tubing behind a boat is really fun on a hot, summer day.
5. Willy's tennis ball rolled under the couch.
6. The large box was too heavy for the delivery person to pick up.

Lesson 1.20, page 51

too	very	practically	politely	freshly	carefully
lately	quite	initially	mostly	generously	grumpily
originally	outside	desperately	quickly	icily	obviously
only	barely	much	so	reluctantly	

AWV. Some possible answers are below.

Very early Tuesday morning, Travis's alarm rang loudly. The noise startled him from a mostly deep sleep. He was initially annoyed, but then he happily remembered why he had to wake so early. Today, Travis would begin generously volunteering at the local food pantry. The pantry helpfully provided meals for those in need. The breakfast shift was especially important. A child could get a freshly made breakfast before heading to school. Travis quickly dressed and rushed carefully down the stairs. The sun barely peaked above the horizon, so the sky was mostly still dark. Travis had originally planned to bike to the pantry, because it was not too far from his apartment. Then, he looked outside at the thermometer hanging helpfully near the window. The temperature was icily cold at just 30°! Travis practically shivered at the thought of riding in such freezing weather. Instead, he trudged reluctantly back up the stairs and tapped gently at his much older brother's door. He heard Aaron grumpily ask, "What?" But when he politely explained why he desperately needed a ride, he jumped eagerly out of bed. He was truly impressed with Travis and quite willing to help. It took only a few minutes to drive to the pantry. Travis thanked his brother before heading into the building, a huge grin obviously spreading across his face.

Lesson 1.21, page 52

1. Clare stared more seriously at the treasure map. **2.** The mouse scurried the most quietly across the garage floor. **3.** The International Space Station will be visible sooner. **4.** The service at Mama Mia's Pizza was reviewed more favorably online. **5.** I am most anxiously awaiting my first violin lesson. **6.** Chao yelled most enthusiastically when it was his turn to get on the ride.

Answer Key

Lesson 1.21, page 53

1. more or less excitedly **2.** more or less carefully **3.** more or less angrily **4.** more or less frequently **5.** more or less skillfully **6.** more or less often **7.** most or least gracefully **8.** earlier **9.** later **10.** most or least quickly **11. - 14.** AWV

Lesson 1.22, page 54

1. sudden **2.** suddenly **3.** anxious **4.** anxiously **5.** excitedly **6.** excited **7.** badly **8.** bad

Lesson 1.22, page 55

1. Adj. The pink hydrangeas that Amy brought over looked **stunning.**
2. Adv. Stanley barked **incessantly** at the delivery driver.
3. Adv. The full moon shone **brightly** in the night sky.
4. Adj. The ladder that Mike climbed felt **unstable**, but he used it anyway.
5. Adj. Although we were in a rural area, our cell phone reception was **good.**
6. Adj. Mikhala thought the raw oysters tasted **gross.**
7. Adj. The melody sounded **elegant** as it floated out of the ballroom.
8. Adv. RJ did not do **well** on his flute test for first chair.
9. Adv. The door opened **completely**, and out stepped a seven-foot man.
10. Adv. Olivia made a goal, and her family cheered **wildly** for her.
11. Adj. My grandpa grew **confused** as I tried to explain how to sync his phone to his car.
12. Adj. I became **concerned** after two hours of Aleisha not texting me back.

Lesson 1.23, page 56

AWV. Possible answers include: **1.** on **2.** during **3.** between **4.** over **5.** beneath **6.** around **7.** from **8.** outside

Lesson 1.23, page 57

1. The *Titanic* was going to sail from Southampton, England to New York City. (2)
2. The impressive ship was built in Ireland within three years. (2)
3. Over 2,200 people were on board the *Titanic*. (2)
4. In the *Titanic* first class dining room, guests dined on steak with potatoes, oysters, French cheeses, and more. (3)
5. First class passengers had large rooms above the water line with fancy furniture. (2)
6. Third class passengers had rooms by the loud engines at the bottom of the ship. (3)
7. The *Titanic* was carrying mail and packages over to New York City too. (1)
8. Just before midnight, the *Titanic* hit an iceberg beneath the surface of the water. (3)

E: AWV

Lesson 1.24, page 58

Possible answers: **1.** and **2.** so **3.** because **4.** unless **5.** Neither/nor **6.** but **7.** Whether **8.** Both/and

Lesson 1.24, page 59

Coordinate Conj.: the pink and red tulips; *Correlative Conj.*: either Janelle or Jones, both the concert and the meeting, either in March or April; *Subordinate Conj.*: although I couldn't remember his name, after the wrestling match; **1. - 4.** AWV

Lesson 1.25, page 60

Possible answers: **1.** Ouch **2.** Wow **3.** Phew **4.** Oh **5.** Yay **6.** Oh no; E: Interjections add interest, excitment, and emotion to stories.

Lesson 1.25, page 61

Possible answers: **1.** Oh no! Are you ok? **2.** Yuck! That cheese smells bad! **3.** Yay! I won the lottery! **4.** Wow! You are so smart! **5.** Yes! My mom said I can go to the mall! **6.** Oh! I broke my dad's expensive golf club! **7.** No! I failed my math test! **8.** Ha! That joke is so funny!; E: AWV

Review Lessons 1.18–1.25, pages 62-63

1. ____ The Aztec people were nomadic.
2. ____ Around the year 1300, the Aztecs arrived in what is now central Mexico.
3. ____ They built beautiful temples throughout the region.
4. ____ The temples were large and intricate.
5. S The tallest temple was called Templo Mayor.
6. ____ The temples were religious sites.
7. ____ The Aztec people worshipped many gods.
8. ____ Some words we use today sound similar to words the Aztecs used.
9. C The Aztec civilization lasted longer than 200 years.
10. ____ Many Aztec descendants still live in Mexico today.

As indicated, rewrite each sentence to change the adverb to a comparative or superlative adverb. If the sentence contains an intensifier, circle the intensifier.

11. The raft raced speedily through the rapids.

Superlative: The raft raced most speedily through the rapids.

12. Ms. Simmons was really tired this evening, so she trudged sleepily to her bedroom.

Comparative: Ms. Simmons was really tired this evening, so she trudged more sleepily to her bedroom.

13. bad **14.** sad **15.** well **16.** nervously **17.** sweet **18.** I, **19.** P, behind the shed, **20.** C **21.** P, until his car is fixed **22.** C **23. - 26.** AWV

Answer Key

Review Chapter 1, pages 64-65

1. A common noun names a general noun and is not capitalized. A proper noun names a specific noun and is capitalized. **2.** AWV **3.** Problem: There is a pronoun shift; Correct: Our principal always says that if a student wants to succeed, he/she must put in the work. **4.** Problem: The subject and verb do not agree; Correct: The people who live in our neighborhood asked me to shovel their driveway while they are gone. **5.** make, made; did, will do; wake, will wake; begin, began **6.** most exciting (S) **7.** burned (P) **8.** angrier (P) **9.** hotter (C) **10.** more expensive (C) **11.** gently, how **12.** yesterday, when **13.** confidently, how; intensifier: quite **14.** up the hill, in the anthill, but **15.** in the car, Since **16.** in the downpour, Both/and **17.** to the Mayan ruins, While **18.** in the sweltering heat, yet

Lesson 2.1, page 68

1. Is the weather in the eye of a hurricane calm? **2.** Wow, the eye of a hurricane can span 20-40 miles wide! **3.** Tell me a little bit about hurricanes. **4.** A category 2 hurricane is dangerous. **5.** Major hurricanes are ones with winds over 110mph. **6.** Do ocean temperatures need to be above 79°F for a hurricane to form?

Lesson 2.1, page 69

First paragraph: IM, IN, IN, IN, IN, D, D, D, D, IN, D, E; Second paragraph: D, D, IM, IN, D, D, D; Third paragraph: IN, D, D, D, D, D, E, D, IN, E, D; E: AWV

Lesson 2.2, page 70

1. c **2.** e **3.** d **4.** a **5.** b

Lesson 2.2, page 71

1. C, S: 2, P: 2; **2.** C, S: 3, P: 2; **3.** S, S: 1, P: 2; **4.** C, S: 2, P: 2; **5.** C, S: 2, P: 2; **6.** S, S: 1, P: 2; E: AWV

Lesson 2.3, page 72

Possible answers: **1.** When she gets home, **2.** while we played a game inside. **3.** because she is planting new ones. **4.** once he heard thunder in the distance. **5.** unless it is storming. **6.** Once class was dismissed,

Lesson 2.3, page 73

1. although most people refer to it as "The Bean." **2.** When you are in Chicago **3.** While some visitors stand close to it **4.** until he moved to Britain in the early 1970s **5.** Once when I visited The Bean **6.** Because of its arched shape **7.** because of its shape **8.** Since The Bean is in Millennium Park **9. - 12.** AWV

Lesson 2.4, page 74

1. which **2.** when **3.** When **4.** If **5.** that **6.** who

Lesson 2.4, page 75

1. which live near the Sahara Desert **2.** that has very hot and dry conditions **3.** that offer shelter from the sun **4.** which hunt in packs of 15 to 60 **5.** While most wild dogs share a long, thin body **6.** that give it an acute sense of hearing **7.** that are extremely vocal **8.** Although they bear a resemblance to domesticated dogs
E: AWV

Review Chapter 2, pages 76-77

1. IN **2.** E **3.** D **4.** E **5.** D **6.** E **7.** IN **8.** IM **9.** S **10.** C **11.** C **12.** C **13.** S **14.** C **15.** Although our flight was delayed **16.** Whenever my cousin goes swimming **17.** after we stop at the Statue of Liberty **18.** Unless you brought sunscreen with you **19.** when she has a stomachache **20.** while her dad went into the grocery store **21.** which are tall, thin dogs **22.** Although greyhounds are large dogs **23.** Even though greyhounds are known for their racing **24.** which is the fastest dog breed in the world **25.** that are sensitive to temperature changes **26.** Because they are often surrendered when they can't race anymore **27. - 28.** AWV

Lesson 3.1, page 80

1. "Did anyone feed Bubbles?" asked Mom. **2.** "When you get home," said Leticia, "please tell Mom that I'm staying for gymnastics practice." **3.** "The tree blew over on our shed," said Dad. "I'll call tomorrow to have it removed." **4.** "We're going to the gym in ten minutes!" yelled Padma. "Does anyone want to come?"; E: Correct punctuation in dialogue helps a reader see where sentences begin and end.
E: AWV

Lesson 3.1, page 81

1. b **2.** c **3.** a **4.** a **5.** c; E: AWV

Lesson 3.2, page 82

Heading: 1879 Fruitvale Road, Hot Springs, Arkansas 76212 June 2, 2023; Salutation: Dear Elijah,; Closing: Your friend, Trudy

Lesson 3.2, page 83

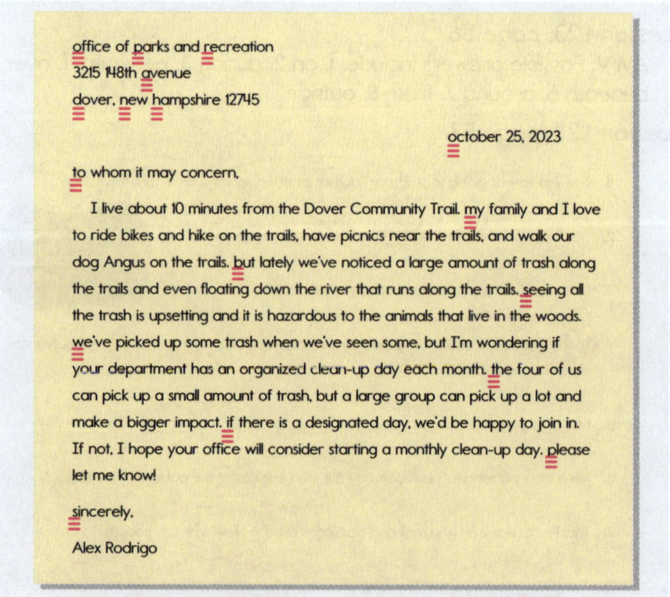
office of parks and recreation
3215 148th avenue
dover, new hampshire 12745

october 25, 2023

to whom it may concern,

I live about 10 minutes from the Dover Community Trail. my family and I love to ride bikes and hike on the trails, have picnics near the trails, and walk our dog Angus on the trails. but lately we've noticed a large amount of trash along the trails and even floating down the river that runs along the trails. seeing all the trash is upsetting and it is hazardous to the animals that live in the woods. we've picked up some trash when we've seen some, but I'm wondering if your department has an organized clean-up day each month. the four of us can pick up a small amount of trash, but a large group can pick up a lot and make a bigger impact. if there is a designated day, we'd be happy to join in. If not, I hope your office will consider starting a monthly clean-up day. please let me know!

sincerely,

Alex Rodrigo

E: Without correct capitalization, it is difficult to know where one sentence ends and another begins.

Lesson 3.3, page 84

1. - 5. AWV

Answer Key

Lesson 3.3, page 85

Have you ever been to our nation's capital? If not, washington, dc, should be on your list of places to visit. There is so much to see and do in this bustling, beautiful district that borders virginia and maryland. The Metro will take you all around the city, from the national museum of american history to the smithsonian national zoo. And best of all, many of the most popular sights, like the lincoln memorial and jefferson memorial, are free to visit!

Are you interested in space exploration? If so, the air and space museum is for you! Here, you can see the wright flyer, which was the first airplane built by orville and wilbur wright. You can also see charles lindbergh's spirit of st. louis, which was the first aircraft to fly nonstop from new york to paris. Also in this museum is neil armstrong's spacesuit that he wore on the apollo 17 mission. You could spend all day in this museum!

Would you like to see where george and martha washington lived? Just outside of washington, dc, is their historic estate called mount vernon. situated beautifully on the potomac river, the breathtaking grounds include the mansion, gardens, a riding stable, slave memorial, smoke house, ice house, and more. This 500-acre estate in virginia, as well as famous landmarks like the capitol in washington, dc, should be on everyone's list of places to visit in and around our nation's capital.

Lesson 3.4, page 86

1. French **2.** East Coast **3.** Lions Club **4.** Detroit Lions **5.** Industrial Revolution **6.** Department of Agriculture

Lesson 3.4, page 87

1. Revolutionary War **2.** AWV **3.** Supreme Court **4.** Bill of Rights **5.** Civil War, Gettysburg Address **6.** World War II (WWII) **7.** AWV **8.** Russian **9.** Apple **10.** AWV; E: AWV

Review Chapter 3, pages 88-89

1. Mika grew up on the west coast, but after College he moved to New Hampshire.
2. Vicki is italian, although she does not speak the Language fluently.
3. Mrs. chang's first article appeared in *photography today* magazine.
4. My Aunt bought my favorite cereal called green earth granola.
5. To reach the wilton museum of arts and crafts, turn West on broad street.
6. Did you know that six Presidents have been named James?
7. Donita plans to be a Doctor someday, but she hasn't decided on a specialty yet.
8. Did you know that portuguese is the official language of brazil?
9. Mom doesn't follow professional sports, but she's a big fan of the carolina tarheels.
10. Next summer, the kim family plans to visit grand canyon national park in arizona.

11. ✓ **12.** X **13.** X **14.** X **15.** ✓ **16.** ✓ **17.** ✓ **18.** X **19.** Spanish **20.** Senate **21.** Mayor **22.** *Emma*

Learning Checkpoint Chapters 1–3, pages 90-95

1. Costa Rica **2.** South **3.** country's **4.** it unique **5.** which **6.** see them **7.** who sees **8.** itself, **9.** animals' **10.** Tortuguero National Park **11.** eat **12.** will go **13.** smells/looks, has the linking verb **14.** To mow (I) **15.** humming (P) **16.** Talking (G) **17.** modified (P) **18.** watch, bake (present) **19.** added (past) **20.** will be done (future) **21.** scratchy, predicate **22.** weakest, superlative **23.** Italian, proper **24.** softer, comparative **25.** early/late, very/really **26.** too **27.** loudly **28.** below **29.** outside **30.** As long as, into **31.** E **32.** IN **33.** D **34.** IM **35.** simple **36.** complex **37.** compound **38.** complex **39.** that is too small for our family of five, adjective **40.** When I have enough money saved up, adverb **41.** a **42.** c **43.** c **44.** Community Mental Health 12263 Collin Avenue Plainfield, Illinois 60544 **45.** August 1, 2023 **46.** To whom it may concern, **47.** Regards, **48.** X **49.** ✓ **50.** ✓ **51.** X **52.** ✓ **53.** X, X **54.** X **55.** ✓ **56.** X **57.** ✓

Lesson 4.1, page 98

1. (.) **2.** (!) **3.** (!) **4.** (.) **5.** (.) **6.** (?) **7.** (?) **8.** (.)

Lesson 4.1, page 99

1. (.) **2.** (?) **3.** (.) **4.** (.) or (!) **5.** (?) **6.** (.) **7.** (.) **8.** (?) **9.** (!) **10.** (.) **11.** (.) or (!); E: Ending punctuation can tell us if a sentence is asking a question, stating something with strong emotion, or just making a statement or command.

Lesson 4.2, page 100

1. thunder, lightning, and hail **2.** big, burly **3.** ✓ **4.** eggs, bacon, hashbrowns, and a donut **5.** ✓ **6.** a coin, a ring, and some keys

Lesson 4.2, page 101

1. (a) gardening, crafting, and scrapbooking **2.** (b)large, open conference room **3.** (c) **4.** (a) weeding, planting, and fertilizing **5.** (c) **6.** (b) Very creative, enthusiastic people **7.** (a) Monday, Tuesday, and Thursday **8.** (a) photography, sketching, and painting; E: AWV

Lesson 4.3, page 102

1. Moxie, come back here!
2. If you know the answer, DiMarco, raise your hand.
3. I ordered you a thin-crust veggie pizza, Ally.
4. Carlos, do you want to go to the park after school?
5. Have I ever led you astray before, Dom?
6. Mr. Llewellyn, have you graded my paper yet?
7. If you have a moment, Emry, I'd like to speak with you.
8. Congratulations, Jon, you earned first chair in the saxophone section.

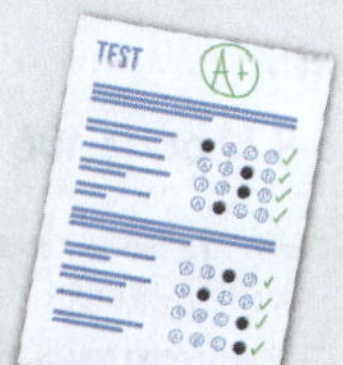

E: AWV

Lesson 4.4, page 103

1. Your friend, **2.** June 7, 2023 **3.** I have a degree in Biology, and I am very interested in applying for this job. **4.** Sincerely, **5.** San Francisco, CA 94109 **6.** When we visited my grandma, we took cookies to her. **7.** Dear Aunt Rachael, **8.** All my love, **9.** December 23, 2023 **10.** Charlotte, NC 28201

Answer Key

Lesson 4.5, page 104

1. X Kenya is in East Africa, which is on the Indian Ocean.
2. X Although part of its landscape is a savanna, it also has mountains and plateaus.
3. X There are more than 60 languages spoken in Kenya, and almost everyone speaks more than one.
4. X Because Kenya is home to so many beautiful animal species, the government has established more than 50 reserves to protect them.
5. C Because bones of one of the earliest human ancestors were found in Kenya, scientists wonder if humans originated here.
6. C During the 1600s and 1700s, many Kenyans were taken as enslaved people by Americans, Europeans, and Arabs.

E: AWV

Lesson 4.5, page 105

Have you visited Niagara Falls? If you haven't, you should see this natural wonder. Niagara Falls isn't just one waterfall, it is three humongous waterfalls. There are two waterfalls on the American side, and one waterfall on the Canadian side. Because each one is beautiful in its own way, you should really see all three.

Niagara Falls was formed by glaciers melting during the last Ice Age, which was around 12,000 years ago. Over 700,000 gallons of water per second flow over the falls which makes it the largest waterfall in North America in volume. If you measured its speed, the water rushes at 25 miles per hour!

All of this powerful, rushing water is put to good use thanks to Nikola Tesla and George Westinghouse. They created the world's first hydroelectric power plant that uses the water to generate electricity! The water from Niagara Falls generates 4 million kilowatts of electricity, which powers a quarter of the state of New York and Ontario, Canada.

People have plunged over the falls on purpose, but most have not survived. Fish often flow over the falls with the water, and they have a higher survival rate than humans.

If you plan to visit these stunning falls, bring a camera and a raincoat. The spray from the falls often gives visitors a cool shower.

E: AWV

Lesson 4.6, page 106

1. "Grab your pencils," said our teacher, "we are going to take a short quiz."
2. "I haven't read any of the chapters that were assigned," Jalen said nervously.
3. "This unit is so hard," said Malek.
4. "If I pass this quiz," said Rosy, "it'll be a miracle"
5. Trent smirked, "Maybe you all should have paid more attention in class"
6. "I have paid attention," said Anton, "but chemistry is so confusing."
7. "And Mrs. Bultman talks so fast, it's hard to keep up with my notes," said Bella.
8. "You have thirty minutes for the quiz," said Mrs. Bultman, "and you can get started now."

E: AWV

Lesson 4.6, page 107

DeShaun walked out to the pool where his dad was reading a book.

"Hey Dad, what are you doing?" he asked.

Looking up from his book, he replied, "Reading a book."

Laughing, DeShaun said, "I can see that, but I meant, what are you reading?"

"I'm reading a book about World War II," said his dad. "A young Italian boy is forced to spy on Hitler and his men. He learns about what they have planned and then brings back this information to the Italian government. He speaks Italian and German, so he's a perfect spy."

"Wow," said DeShaun, "that sounds really good. Is it a true story?"

"It is," said his dad, "which makes it even more interesting. I'm about halfway through it and I can't wait to see what happens."

"Can I borrow it when you're done," asked DeShaun "because I am looking for a new book to read?"

"Yes! If I get some alone time by the pool, I'll finish it faster," he said with a smirk.

"Oh, I get it," laughed DeShaun. "I'll go find someone else to talk to."

E: Correct punctuation tells a reader where sentences begin and end, who is talking, where a reader should pause, etc.

Review Lessons 4.1–4.6, pages 108-109

1. (?) **2.** (!) **3.** (.) **4.** (.) **5.** (?)

1764 Echo St.
Des Moines, IA 50301
July 31, 2023

Mrs. Laura Santiago
7609 Coaster Rd.
Iowa City, IA 52240

Dear Mrs. Santiago:

I am writing to you today to thank you, your lifeguards, and your emergency response team for helping my family on our most recent trip to your amusement park. It was a hot, sunny day and temperatures were well into the 90s. While waiting in line for the Screamin' Sally waterslide, my dad felt lightheaded. He fell to the hot concrete ground, hit his head, and got a big, nasty bump on his forehead. Many concerned people gathered around. Your response team raced over, gently placed him on a big, long stretcher, and started administering first aid. Once they gave him water, helped him cool down, and got him back on his feet, he felt much better. Your team helped turn a scary, unexpected event into an experience that turned out okay. Thank you!

Sincerely,
Tatum White

6. Kevin, do you want to meet in the park later today? **7.** "We fly out at 6am," said Alana, "so we have to get up really early." **8.** My dog is scared of the water, so we don't take him to the beach. **9.** ✓ **10.** Please take the trash out when you leave, Reagan. **11.** Because of the extreme drought, we can't water our grass every day. **12.** ✓ **13.** "Look out!" yelled Marty. "Caleb has a 90mph pitch!" **14.** Since I didn't do well on my first test, I will retake the test next week. **15.** I was really tired last night, yet I couldn't fall asleep for hours. **16.** "What time is your cross country practice today?" asked my dad.

Lesson 4.7, page 110

1. over night; by morning, **2.** the following items on it: **3.** deleted a notebook app; I washed my car; and I read two chapters in my new book. **4.** at the coffee shop: Ed Sheeran.

Answer Key

Lesson 4.7, page 111

1. are lions, elephants, wildebeests, and giraffes. **2.** grasslands; the grasses **3.** all year long; they have **4.** looking for food; this is called migration. **5.** in many ways: they stop overcrowding **6.** desertification; this is bad **7.** special survival traits: elephants and giraffes **8.** the world's largest savanna: the Serengeti in Africa.

Lesson 4.8, page 112

1. "Can you tell me again," asked Mr. Brooks, "which schools will be marching in the parade?" **2.** Marcus reminded me, "Mrs. Greenwood said, 'You'll all have two tries on the experiment. If the first one fails, you can redo it.'" **3.** My cousins and I love singing "Grandma Got Run Over by a Reindeer" around the holidays. **4.** "Janie, the receptionist said, 'Arrive 15 minutes before your appointment to fill out new-patient paperwork,'" said my mom. **5.** "The poem 'Be Glad Your Nose Is on Your Face' by Jack Prelutsky makes me laugh," said Wilbur.
E: AWV

Lesson 4.8, page 113

My English teacher Mr. Taylor said, "Let's talk about poems today. Who has a favorite poem that they'd like to tell us the title of?"

Miriam raised her hand and replied, "My favorite poem is from Shel Silverstein's book Where the Sidewalk Ends. It's called the 'Homework Machine.'"

"Thank you, Miriam. That's a funny one," said Mr. Taylor. "Jesse, you have your hand up. What poem is your favorite?" he asked.

"My favorite poem is 'Jabberwocky' by Lewis Carroll. It's full of nonsense words that are almost impossible to memorize," he said.

"Oh yes," said Mr. Taylor. "I had to recite part of 'Jabberwocky' for an acting class I took when I was young. That is a difficult one."

"My mom told me, 'If you can memorize and recite the entire poem to me, I'll take you out to lunch,'" said Jesse. "I did it and she took me to our favorite Mexican restaurant."

"Wow, that's great," said Mr. Taylor. "Would you like to recite it to the class?" he asked.

"That was last year," said Jesse. "I don't even think I'd remember the first line," he said, laughing.

E: AWV

Lesson 4.9, page 114

1. ✓ **2.** X **3.** X **4.** ✓ **5.** X **6.** ✓

Lesson 4.9, page 115

1. Farmers across the country use cows' manure as fertilizer.
2. What you probably haven't heard, though, is that manure can be used to create power.
3. With a single cow producing about 30 gallons of manure a day, that's a lot of manure!
4. Scientists' idea of using manure to create power is brilliant.
5. The manure's dropped in a giant tank called a digester.
6. The digester's job is to collect gas that is given off by the manure, which can be turned into energy.
7. If a farmer's crops don't do well one year, they can sell their manure energy.
8. Cow manure energy isn't a fossil fuel, so it's not harmful to the environment.

E: AWV

Lesson 4.10, page 116

1. sister-in-law, self-described **2.** twenty-two, in-side **3.** far-fetched **4.** mind-blowing, sur-prised **5.** up-to-date

Lesson 4.10, page 117

1. great-grandmother, much-loved **2.** well-worn, ninety-five **3.** above-average **4.** well-stocked, over-the-counter **5.** knee-slapping **6.** clean-cut **7.** thirty-one, twenty-five-dollar **8.** not-so-patient, merry-go-round **9.** - **10.** AWV

Lesson 4.11, page 118

1. –which is common along the coast of Maine– **2.** –I need to apologize to my friend. **3.** –and I've thought about this for a while– **4.** –who started out in country music– **5.** –he needs to go to the vet.

Lesson 4.11, page 119

1. –which I can't– **2.** –known as the "King of Rock and Roll"– **3.** –even though he's on vacation– **4.** –a trick scooter. **5.** –a chocolate mint milkshake. **6.** –St. Andrews.

Lesson 4.12, page 120

1. At 119° F (48° C), **2.** (HBCUs) **3.** (January 6, 2021) **4.** (that I deleted) **5.** (because they have the best BBQ)

Lesson 4.12, page 121

1. - **6.** AWV; E: Parentheses are used in informal writing as a way of calling attention to information or interrupting a sentence.

Lesson 4.13, page 122

1. National Geographic Kids **2.** Prisoner B-3087 **3.** Wheel of Fortune **4.** Hamilton **5.** Who Is Rosa Parks? **6.** Mission Impossible **7.** Survivor **8.** USA Today; E: Titles of works are italicized or underlined to call special attention to them in text.

Lesson 4.13, page 123

1. - **8.** AWV

Review Lessons 4.7–4.13, pages 124-125

1. (:) **2.** (:) **3.** (;) **4.** (;) **5.** "If I had ridden my bike faster, I wouldn't have gotten rained on," said Azul. **6.** "Kaitlyn, my mom can't give you a ride home today," said Lyle. **7.** "The doctor said, 'You won't be able to run track until your ankle heals,'" said Anna. **8.** "I think I want to join the boys' swim team this winter," said Rico. **9.** "Lucy's skis and poles went flying everywhere!" yelled her friend, Dana. **10.** The boy's quick throw to first base finally ended the game. **11.** Mr. Reynolds won a well-deserved award-Teacher of the Year. **12.** For my mom's thirty-ninth birthday (May 15), my dad took her to her favorite restaurant. **13.** My much-loved cardinals destroyed the carefully built birdhouse that I made for them. **14.** Izzy had her paws on the windowsill (the windowsill of our front window) watching the delivery person park at the end of our driveway. **15.** We tried to get our dog (his name is Steve) to go swimming on vacation. **16.** My rule-following uncle always drives the strictly enforced speed limit (25 mph). **17.** Blackish, **18.** Brian's Winter **19.** The Lion King **20.** Barbie

Answer Key

Review Chapter 4, pages 126-127

Across: 1. conjunction 3. interrogative 5. colon 6. italics 8. quotation 9. hyphen

Down: 1. complex 2. salutation 4. apostrophes 7. comma

1. We read To Kill a Mockingbird in class before watching the movie.
2. What is your favorite book-turned-movie, Carly?
3. Marco's Lawn Service does it all: weeding, fertilizing, planting, and cutting.
4. My well-intentioned grandmother bought me a book on hygiene called Guy Stuff, The Body Book for Boys.
5. I can't imagine what it must be like to live in Hawai'i—how cool!
6. Yay, our class won the can-collecting contest!
7. I didn't find Lawrence's backpack in the boys' restroom.
8. "You have twenty-five minutes for the test," said Mr. Brown, "and not a minute more."
9. Salzburg, which is in Austria, is the birthplace of Wolfgang Amadeus Mozart (one of the greatest composers in history).
10. Wear your black rubber boots into the garden when you go out to pick tomatoes, peppers, and beans.
11. My answer was no; I didn't feel that a ten-year-old should be going to a late-night movie.
12. "Arlo, share your candy with your cute baby sister," said my mom. "If you don't, she's going to start crying."

Lesson 5.1, page 130

1. MM 2. DM 3. ✓ 4. MM 5. MM 6. DM; E: AWV

Lesson 5.1, page 131

AWV. Possible answers include: 1. As she was skateboarding to the park, Lindsey saw a deer. 2. Since I was almost nine years old, my mom thought it was time for me to start making my bed. 3. The bus still pulled away without Ben even though he sprinted to the bus stop. 4. As he was running out the door, Jacob promised to wash the dishes. 5. As we were biking over the bridge, a freighter suddenly appeared. 6. While we were swimming in the lake, the rip currents were getting worse.

Lesson 5.2, page 132

1. anywhere 2. anyone 3. any 4. anything 5. anywhere; E: AWV

Lesson 5.2, page 133

1. won't eat any 2. Don't anyone 3. can hardly 4. didn't care about anything 5. not going anywhere 6. wasn't anybody 7. haven't ever 8. doesn't want anything

Lesson 5.3, page 134

AWV. Possible answers include: 1. The cashier was very friendly. 2. My dentist with the red hair and nice smile is friendly. 3. Lola quit her job because she had to be home more to help care for her grandmother. 4. Jamal chose the Strikers soccer camp because it was inexpensive. 5. Mother's Day is in May.

Lesson 5.3, page 135

AWV. Possible answers include: 1. My aunt and uncle live near Buffalo, New York. 2. At 3:30pm, I saw a black dog chasing a white dog. 3. Supposedly, children can learn how to tie their shoes around the age of four. 4. ✓ 5. The morning announcement told us to expect a fire drill later today. 6. The best golfer will win a spot on the team. E: Writing that is too wordy can confuse a reader, it can introduce unknown words to a reader, and it can interfere with the flow of a paragraph or story.

Lesson 5.4, page 136

1. cross off: free 2. cross off: true 3. cross off: at night 4. cross off: in length 5. cross off: briefly 6. cross off: again

Lesson 5.4, page 137

1. dead, already mentions that the mosquitoes will be killed 2. basic, essentials are basics 3. happy or joyful, they are synonyms 4. in the morning, already states am (for morning) 5. again, return means *to come back again* 6. in length, longer implies length; E: Concise sentences are easier to read and understand than sentences that have redundancies in them.

Review Chapter 5, pages 138-139

1. (DM), As the skater raced ever closer toward the goalie, he lost the puck just inches from the goal 2. (DM), While Maddie skateboarded to the park, she saw a fire truck scream by. 3. (MM), As he glanced out the window, my dog spied a raccoon. 4. (MM), On Sunday our Aunt Shania said she would call us. 5. (MM), I saw the helicopter as I was looking out over the lake. 6. (DM) As I was boarding the plane, a crying baby caught my eye. 7. I didn't yell at anyone. 8. Leila couldn't find anywhere to park. 9. I don't have any ice for the cooler. 10. The avocado wasn't good anymore. 11. The classroom rules have been established for the safety of all. 12. Maleek lied to make me believe he made the basketball team. 13. My grandma made us dinner since my mom had to work late and my dad was out of town for work. 14. new, never-before-heard, 7pm in the evening 15. protested against 16. declare a statement, dinner meal 17. cash money, ATM machine, 18. surrounded on all sides 19. returns again 20. frozen ice

Lesson 6.1, page 142

Possible answers: 1. predict 2. credit 3. captain 4. deduct 5. telegraph 6. describe 7. structure 8. contact 9. unicycle 10. thermometer 11. geography 12. automated

Lesson 6.1, page 143

1. strength 2. seize 3. build 4. draw 5. bend 6. peace 7. death 8. say 9. change 10. - 11. AWV

Lesson 6.2, page 144

1. untied 2. misunderstand 3. interact 4. nonsensible 5. overload 6. rediscover 7. misdiagnose 8. antifreeze 9. preregister 10. immature

Lesson 6.3, page 145

Across: 2. usable 4. walkable 6. conversation 8. thoughtless 9. suspenseful 10. poetic

Down: 1. meaningless 3. straighten 5. randomly 7. collector

Lesson 6.4, page 146

Possible answers: 1. request 2. early 3. night 4. confessed, dangerous 5. more 6. reveal 7. sharp 8. straight

Lesson 6.4, page 147

1. start 2. wide 3. bother 4. determine 5. chop 6. chilly 7. complicated 8. instructions 9. untrue 10. west 11. enemy 12. join 13. hope 14. ancient 15. bitter 16. clumsy 17. general 18. captive 19. pessimism 20. error 21. deny 22. greedy

Lesson 6.5, page 148

1. Greece 2. groan 3. allowed, to 4. coarse 5. grate 6. led, where 7. ceiling, their 8. build

E: AWV

Answer Key

Lesson 6.5, page 149

"I have good ~~gnus~~ news, Mom," JaLean said to her mom as she walked ~~threw~~ through the door.

"Oh, I can't ~~weight~~ wait to ~~here~~ hear it! I've had a boring day, so I could use ~~sum~~ some good news," her mom replied.

"On the ~~weigh~~ way to get my ~~hare~~ hair cut, I ran into Mr. Lewis. ~~Ewe no~~ You know him. He's my English teacher from this ~~passed~~ past year."

"Yes, I remember him," said JaLeans's mom.

"He told me that he liked the paper that I ~~rote~~ wrote on Ireland ~~sew~~ so much that he wants me to ~~right~~ write for the school newspaper next year."

"That's exciting!" said JaLean's mom. "~~Dew~~ Do you want ~~two~~ to?"

"Of ~~coarse~~ course I want ~~two~~ to!" exclaimed JaLean. "He told me that the writers get to ~~chews~~ choose what to ~~right~~ write about. He said last year there were articles about the ~~whether~~ weather, a local ~~stake~~ steak restaurant, ~~rapping~~ wrapping presents for the holidays, and even an article about our ~~principle~~ principal, Mrs. Teague."

"Sounds like a lot of fun," said her mom. "I'm glad he offered that ~~too~~ to you."

"I feel like I ~~one~~ won the lottery!" laughed JaLean.

Lesson 6.6, page 150

Possible sentences: **1.** I learned how to use a bow and arrow. **2.** My science teacher conducted an experiment in class. **3.** Politics is a subject that is off-limits in my house. **4.** You should deposit your birthday money in the bank. **5.** We saw a black bear on the trail! **6.** Did you enter the contest? E: Context clues and surrounding words can help you figure out which homograph is being used in a sentence.

Lesson 6.6, page 151

b	n	o	v	e	l	c	j	w	e	s	g	l
g	a	k	c	o	t	d	m	e	p	a	r	s
p	w	a	l	c	h	e	l	n	r	o	c	n
m	a	p	t	h	a	f	i	m	o	p	e	d
v	t	o	c	g	w	e	v	i	j	o	w	a
a	c	p	k	r	o	c	k	n	e	m	i	l
n	h	w	a	s	q	t	s	o	c	s	n	c
l	r	k	s	u	s	p	e	c	t	i	d	t

1. an imperfection; to forsake a cause or nation due to a change in thought
   d e f e c t
2. an instrument that is worn and tells time; to look at
   w a t c h
3. to move back and forth; a piece of earth
   r o c k
4. something specific to work on; to display outwardly
   p r o j e c t
5. a movement of air; to wrap something around an object
   w i n d
6. someone thought to be involved in a crime; to have doubts
   s u s p e c t
7. new; a book
   n o v e l
8. to be sad; a small motorbike
   m o p e d

Lesson 6.7, page 152

Possible answers: *Positive:* smile, natural, gaze, genius, chef, officer, vintage; *Neutral:* aggressive, slender, plain, smart, cook, cop, inexpensive, sad, young, overweight, old; *Negative:* smirk, pushy, scrawny, stare, cheap, depressed, immature, obese

Lesson 6.7, page 153

1. inquisitive **2.** unique **3.** collects **4.** wild **5.** stingy **6.** liar **7.** private **8.** immature; E: Choosing words carefully is important because synonyms can have different connotations, which could alter the meaning of your writing.

Lesson 6.8, page 154

1. Mr. Reinick's classroom, zoo (metaphor) **2.** Rex, dictionary (metaphor) **3.** Liam, peaks (simile) **4.** ghost pepper, fire (simile) **5.** computer lab, dinosaurs (metaphor) **6.** life, dream (simile) **7.** banana peel, sun (simile)

Lesson 6.8, page 155

1. - 10. AWV

Lesson 6.9, page 156

1. b **2.** b **3.** d **4.** c **5.** c **6.** a

Lesson 6.9, page 157

Possible answers: **1.** Los Angeles **2.** fish **3.** November **4.** dye **5.** violin **6.** dry **7.** hockey **8.** thermometer **9. - 10.** AWV

Lesson 6.10, page 158

1. Prince Charming **2.** much ado about nothing **3.** Trojan horse **4.** as gullible as Alice **5.** kryptonite **6.** cried wolf **7.** Herculean task **8.** Tiger Woods of miniature golf; E: Including allusions adds variety and interest to writing.

Lesson 6.10, page 159

1. Mother Teresa, a noble woman who mothered orphaned children **2.** Cicero, one of the greatest speakers (orators) of all time **3.** weight of the world on his shoulders, Greek god Atlas who carried the world on his shoulders **4.** Romeo to your Juliet, Shakespearean love story **5.** click her heels and be back home, Dorothy in The Wizard of Oz **6.** Titan, Greek gods who were very large

Lesson 6.11, page 160

1. pie was calling my name **2.** cool water touched my feet **3.** time flies **4.** alarm clock yells **5.** brakes on Amelio's car whined **6.** strip in Las Vegas is alive and kicking **7.** winds howled **8.** thirsty flowers **9.** story jumped **10.** old tree groaned **11.** engine roared to life **12.** blanket hugged

Lesson 6.11, page 161

AWV; E: Personification adds human characteristics to non-human things, which can make writing more interesting, descriptive, and fun to read.

Review Chapter 6, pages 162-163

1. AWV: predict, dictation, **2.** AWV: construction, instruct **3.** one who, AWV **4.** again, AWV **5.** characterized by or tending to, AWV **6.** wrongly, AWV **7.** without, AWV **8.** not or opposite of, AWV **9.** c **10.** a **11.** f **12.** e **13.** d **14.** b **15.** polar bear **16.** Washington **17.** yawning **18.** February **19.** cereal **20.** cymbal **21.** dense **22.** muscle **23.** M **24.** P **25.** S **26.** A

Answer Key

Learning Checkpoint Chapters 4–6, pages 164-169

1. interrogative **2.** declarative, imperative **3.** exclamatory, imperative **4.** (?) **5.** (!) **6.** (.) **7.** (!) **8.** responsible, conscientious **9.** breakfast, she **10.** Rowan, **11.** the post office, the grocery store, and the bank **12.** tall, glorious **13.** running, and **14.** the Bloodhound, the Standard Poodle, and the Wire Fox Terrier. **15.** The boys' hockey team is going to the state finals; it'll be an amazing game. **16.** "Keisha," said Mrs. Brooks, "you're the runner-up of the weekly math contest!" **17.** Bryn couldn't fit these items in her closet: her saxophone, her boots, and her folded-up chair. **18.** I have twenty-five dollars for the book fair; I'm going to look for these items: a mystery book, a graphic novel, and a keychain. **19.** "Your science teacher said, 'Olive is a great leader in our class,'" said her mom at dinner. **20.** My grandpa turned the wrong way down a one-way street; he did a U-turn so we wouldn't be going the wrong way. **21.** We were laughing loudly as the movie ended. **22.** I served Deion's birthday cake on paper plates to the kids. **23.** Looking out onto Lake Michigan, I saw a big storm brewing. **24.** The sun was setting as I was jogging over the bridge. **25.** either **26.** any **27.** anywhere **28.** im-pass-able **29.** en-joy-able **30.** im-patient-ly **31.** dis-respect-ful **32.** mis-communica-tion **33.** constructed **34.** antique/vintage **35.** crooked **36.** destroyed/ruined **37.** Some **38.** won **39.** sale **40.** tail **41.** AWV **42.** AWV **43.** a heart of gold (M) **44.** as red as a lobster (S) **45.** a pain in the neck (M) **46.** as hard as a rock (S) **47.** b **48.** c **49.** a **50.** c **51.** the bed groaned (P) **52.** act like a Scrooge (A) **53.** sun played hide and seek (P) **54.** my Achilles' heel (A)**55.** - **56.** AWV

Final Test, pages 170-181

1. abstract **2.** collective **3.** proper **4.** common **5.** collective **6.** abstract **7.** houses' **8.** kids' **9.** truck's **10.** mens' **11.** itself **12.** myself **13.** prefer **14.** like **15.** scurry **16.** walks **17.** talks **18.** play **19.** slept **20.** understood **21.** told **22.** thought **23.** strongest **24.** more rambunctious **25.** quietest **26.** most beautiful **27.** quietly **28.** Both/and **29.** carefully **30.** extremely **31.** Since **32.** rather **33.** c **34.** d. **35.** f **36.** a **37.** b **38.** e **39.** ADJ **40.** ADV **41.** ADV **42.** ADJ **43.** I **44.** C **45.** I

46. The affordable care act was signed into law in 2010 by president Barack Obama.

47. I want to visit the louvre museum in paris, france someday.

48. Alex's aunt works for the Michigan department of natural resources.

49. The Battle of Gettysburg took place in 1863 during the civil war.

50. Byron's family is taking a trip to the east coast.

51. Quarterback Aaron Rodgers left the green bay packers for the new york jets.

52. I like to make sandwiches on french bread.

53. (?) **54.** (.) **55.** (!) **56.** (.) or (!) **57.** b **58.** b **59.** a **60.** a **61.** a **62.** a **63.** park, Miguel, (2) **64.** air, (1) **65.** developer, (1) **66.** time, bag, books, (3) **67.** summer, (1) **68.** (;) **69.** (:) **70.** (;) **71.** (:) **72.** (;) **73.** couldn't **74.** I'll, parents' **75.** teachers', students' **76.** I've, Kai's, dog's **77.** toss-up **78.** short-term **79.** twenty-five, empty-handed, **80.** sister-in-law **81.** Hey, Kiddo **82.** Jeopardy! **83.** The grandfather clock chimed at midnight. **84.** On his way to play practice, Wren saw an owl. **85.** The teacher did not want to repeat her directions. **86.** Don't put any mayonnaise on my turkey sandwich. **87.** When Casey was just one month old, her family got a new dog. **88.** Because of the big ice storm, we won't ever make it out of town. **89.** misbehave **90.** kindness **91.** playful **92.** revisit **93.** reckless **94.** preview **95.** unmotivated **96.** wisely **97.** are the same or similar. **98.** are opposites. **99.** grown **100.** breaks **101.** buy **102.** Peace **103.** to allow **104.** the covering of a tree trunk **105.** the snow is a white blanket (M) **106.** as cold as ice (S) **107.** an early bird (M) **108.** as proud as a peacock (S) **109.** d **110.** c **111.** b **112.** c **113.** P **114.** A **115.** A **116.** P